Final Curtain

Final Curtain

The DeWolfe Family in Theatre, Music and Film

By Richard Tappan
Edited by Jennifer Lee

Peter E. Randall Publisher
Portsmouth, New Hampshire
2016

© 2016 Richard Tappan
All rights reserved.

ISBN: 978-1-937721-39-8
Library of Congress Control Number: 2016958152

Peter E. Randall Publisher
P. O. Box 4726
Portsmouth, New Hampshire 03802
www.perpublisher.com

Cover design by Grace Peirce
Text design by Tim Holtz
Cover (clockwise from upper left): Billy DeWolfe, Mabel Keyes DeWolfe, Billy DeWolfe, Jr., B. B. Keyes

Contents

Author's Preface vii

Editor's Foreword ix

Acknowledgments xii

Chapter 1. The Dramatic Beginning: 1893 1

Chapter 2. The Pan-American Exposition Disaster: 1901 4

Chapter 3. Wedding and Warfare: 1907–1916 6

Chapter 4. Marriage and Two Careers: 1916–1919 10

Chapter 5. Everybody Knows Billy: 1874–1928 15

Chapter 6. Testimonial Dinners and the Great Depression: 1928–1931 . . 19

Chapter 7. *Strange Interlude* (1929) and *Lord of the Flies* (1954) 22

Chapter 8. After Billy: 1932–1936 25

Chapter 9. The Pre-war Years: 1936–1941 28

Chapter 10. Walking Alone: 1941–1950 31

Chapter 11. Billy De Wolfe, Jr., and Hollywood 35

Chapter 12. Barbara DeWolfe and the Bretton Woods Conference: 1944 . . 38

Chapter 13. Return to the East: 1950 41

Chapter 14. Mabel's Last Years: 1951–1958 43

Chapter 15. After Mabel: 1958–2016 49

Contents

Illustrations 52
Appendix: The Spanish Civil War 87
References 89
About the Author... 90

Author's Preface

In 2003, my novel *Voices from Cold River* was completed but still unpublished. It was my first novel. It won honorable mention for the Taylor Award from the University of Tennessee. I had already published several magazine articles, both nonfiction and fiction. For two years, I didn't know what to do with *Voices from Cold River*.

Then I came down with bladder cancer in 2006—very shocking indeed. Sally Tappan, my wife, supported me in many ways. I was a nonsmoker and had had a yearly physical. I had many doctors, retired, moved to Maine, and bought a pretty house built in the 1880s, in Eastport, Maine. To the north you can see Campobello Island, Canada. This small city is far away from the closest hospital in Calais.

I took powerful drugs for the cancer, and half a year later I had a major stroke. I was rushed unconscious to Calais and flown by helicopter to Bangor hospital. The doctors operated and cut off half of my skull, and I almost died. Eight weeks of rehabilitation in the wheelchair followed, and Sally came to the hospital every day without fail. For four years I had difficulty speaking. Writing was not an option. I could not write again because I was having difficulty with speech. That seemed to be the end of *Voices from Cold River*. However, Amanda Tappan Tombarelli, my daughter, had the novel published in 2009. Thanks to Mandy.

With the help of God, I am getting better. Writing is therapeutic. In 2010, I enlisted Professor Jennifer Lee, of the University of New Hampshire, to research with me the lives of my grandfather, Billy DeWolfe, and his wife, Mabel. The biography would be called *Full Circle*. For two years, I wrote in pencil on yellow, lined paper. I am good at history, but my left

Author's Preface

hand remains paralyzed. Ironically, I was left-handed. I'm getting good with my right hand and practicing in my journal.

The major source of the family history was the yearly journals Mabel wrote and which remained in the basement of her house in Squantum, Massachusetts, after her death in 1958 at age sixty-five. At her death, her eldest daughter, my aunt Barbara DeWolfe, was forty years old. She lived there alone until 2001, when the house was sold and she moved to a retirement home, taking with her from the basement the journals, photographs, and other artifacts belonging to her mother. The journals remained unread by Barbara, who, like her mother, saved everything from her own life. This collection was the basis of my research.

The journals, pictures, books, and artifacts are like a puzzle with very little context. I learned a lot about Bertrand Keyes, my great-grandfather, as a person and a very talented player of the cornet. Mabel DeWolfe, my grandmother, was a professional violinist. Now I know Mabel's story. My grandmother greatly influenced me. I remember her well; she died when I was eleven.

In 2012, I learned to use Dragon, a voice-operated system for writing on the computer. Using Dragon, I wrote several drafts from the collected materials. Then Jennifer and I together revised and edited the last draft into a clean document. *Full Circle of Music and Theatre: The DeWolfe Family History* was published in limited numbers for family and friends in August 2014.

For more than five years, Jennifer has been my partner and friend. Together we are a good team and want to make the DeWolfe family known to a wider audience. We hope *Final Curtain* will please and interest you.

Richard Tappan
June 2016
Dover, New Hampshire

Editor's Foreword

As Richard tells you in his preface, in August 2014, after almost four years of working together, we had printed for family members *Full Circle of Music and Theatre: The DeWolfe Family History*. The book you're now holding, *Final Curtain: The DeWolfe Family in Theatre, Music and Film*, is an expanded version for libraries, historical societies, and local historians of the Boston/North Shore area, as well as for those interested in the history of vaudeville and the musicians who provided the music for silent films—especially the women musicians.

When Richard and I began working together in the fall of 2010, I had retired from teaching English at the University of New Hampshire-Manchester and was editing an online undergraduate research journal for the University. Our work together was historical research using the personal diaries, journals, scrapbooks of newspaper articles and programs, letters, photos, and other artifacts collected mainly by Richard's grandmother, Mabel Keyes DeWolfe (1893–1958), a professional musician. Therefore, the sources of some events in this book are family memories and traditions and cannot be otherwise documented.

During her lifetime, Mabel kept meticulous journals in tiny, crowded handwriting, from the year of her marriage to Billy DeWolfe in 1916, to a few days before her death in 1958, in Quincy, Massachusetts (only 1918 is missing). Mabel was a virtuoso violinist from an early age and went on to lead several all-women bands and orchestras as well as a popular string trio. She played for many social events, church programs, and graduations; played in the all-women orchestra for silent films at theatres in Lynn, Massachusetts; and gave lessons at a studio she established. She was one of a

Editor's Foreword

very few professional female musicians. After Billy's death in 1932, she supported herself and two daughters principally with her violin.

Billy DeWolfe (1874–1932), vaudeville comedian and theatre manager, was the better known of the couple and the original focus of the family history. The title of this book comes from a newspaper headline announcing his death: "Death Rings Down Curtain on DeWolfe." However, Mabel's story and that of her father, B. B. Keyes, also a professional musician, emerged and took over as we worked our way through the journals and the folders filled with evidence of her professional life. She kept everything! Unfortunately—and strangely—very little has to do with Billy and his career.

In 1974, Richard published a long article in the *Quincy Patriot Ledger* about his grandfather, Billy. Unfortunately, the research that went into that article is lost. Extremely popular in his day as a personality as well as actor, Billy DeWolfe has been totally eclipsed by his protégé to whom he gave his name. If you search for Billy DeWolfe on the Internet, you will find only Billy (Jones) DeWolfe (1907–1974), who had successful careers in theatre, movies, and TV. He remained a loyal and caring "family member," even after the death of his benefactor, and we call him Billy, Jr.

Richard is interested in history and has created historical contexts for family events. He was an English teacher and drama coach, so we have a chapter comparing the play *Strange Interlude* with the novel *Lord of the Flies*. He is a novelist also and speculates at times about the feelings of the various people in the family story.

The process of researching and writing this book was fascinating. I feel very privileged to be part of this project and of the Tappan family. I admire immensely both Richard and his wife, Sally, for their courage but especially for their lively and never-failing sense of humor. We laughed a lot—and still do.

Jennifer Lee
June 2016
Durham, New Hampshire

Mabel's journals were of varying kinds. At top are the small monthly journals kept in the box labelled 1919. Below on left is the 1917 journal in a leather case. Open next to it is the journal for 1955 until the last entry on November 10, 1957. In such a journal, she could compare the day to the same one in previous years.

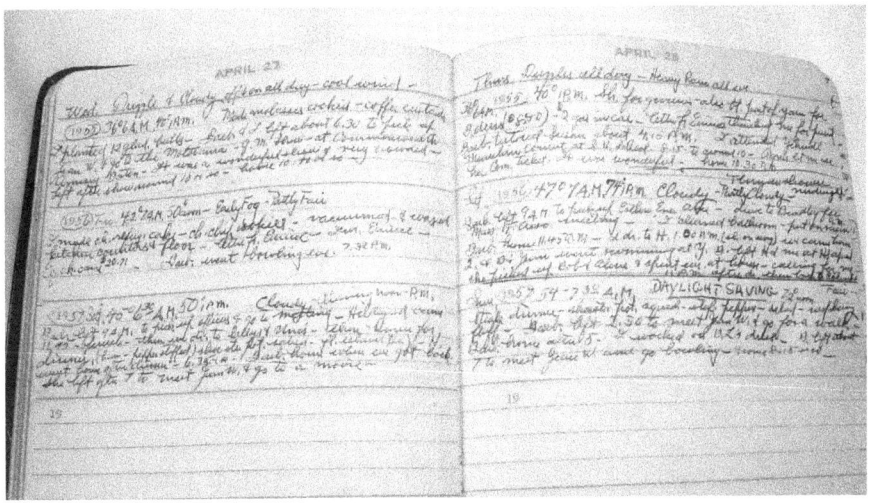

A closer view of Mabel's last journal, 1955 to November, 1957. In her tiny handwriting, she recorded the weather and events of each day, including names of theatre shows or films she saw and the actors in them, along with pieces performed by her various musical groups.

Acknowledgments

My thanks go to Amanda Tappan Tombarelli, my daughter, for technical assistance; to Samuel Tombarelli, my son-in-law, for finding many rare photographs; to Melissa Tappan Parr, my daughter, and to my son-in-law, Andrew Parr, for financing this book; and most of all to Sally Manock Tappan, my wife, for constantly supporting me during the writing of this book. I also want to thank the *Quincy Patriot Ledger* for generously allowing the use of many clippings from its pages. Finally, my sincere appreciation to Deidre Randall, CEO, and Zakariah Johnson, editor, at Peter E. Randall Publisher, for their patient and expert work.

Chapter 1

The Dramatic Beginning
1893

A world's fair, the Columbian Exposition of 1893, held in Chicago, was a triumph of optimism and progress. The White City was brilliant at night, lit by thousands of light bulbs, pure, white, and bright. Bertrand Bernard Keyes was a solo cornetist in the Elgin Cadet Band, playing at the Exposition (figure 1).

The times were rich with possibilities. The late nineteenth century brought many swift transformations. The crowned heads of Europe, including the old queen Victoria, were fixated on the past. Great Britain was at its height of power. However, the United States, more forward-looking, was rapidly developing.

In 1893, Bert was twenty-nine years old and already a well-known musician in Massachusetts. President Grover Cleveland, a Democrat, was in his second term. The planning for the Columbian Exposition began in 1889. The Chicago City Council and the prestigious J. P. Morgan and Charles Schwab organized the big exposition. It was of "immense cultural importance" to America. Twenty-seven million visitors attended the fair, "nearly one quarter of the country's population at the time" ("World's fair," Wikipedia).

The nation's economy was not in good shape in 1893; however, amazingly, the sale of tickets kept on growing. Lyman Gage, bank president; Daniel H. Burnham, architectural director; and many others contributed to the Columbian Exposition. The fair was called the "White City" because of the grand, sparkling buildings and artificial lakes and fountains. Myriads of lights above at night graced the exposition. It was a high point of national fairs, exhibiting a plethora of inventions.

Bertrand Bernard Keyes was born in 1864 in poor circumstances. Samuel Keyes, his father, was a carpenter. When Eliza, his wife, was dying of cancer, they became destitute. In 1875, Samuel took his son to Thompson's Island and "relinquished" him to the Boston Farm and Trade School. The document Samuel Keyes signed said,

> *I am agreeing not to interfere in any manner directly and fully understand the nature of this relinquishment, which is my own free act and deed, made in good faith, solely for the future welfare of the boy. I subscribe my name in the presence of witnesses...*

It was signed Samuel B. Keyes and is dated September 7, 1875 (figure 2).

The Boston Asylum for Indigent Boys had moved to Thompson's Island in Boston Harbor in 1835 to join the Farm School there. The combined schools became the Boston Farm and Trade School. There were two criteria for admittance of a boy to the school: one was poverty or being orphaned; the other was a good character (Stanley 1966).

Bertrand grew up at Thompson's Island until the age of twenty-one. He joined the well-known school band, founded in 1857, and was talented on the cornet. He liked the ocean, but he concentrated on his studies and was an honor student and a leader. He was editor of the school's newspaper, the *Beacon* (figure 3). Then it was 1881, his last year, and Bertrand, now known as B. B., was proud of having a "family" at the school.

In 1875, when B. B. was eleven and admitted to the school, kerosene and gas lights were common. The following year, Alexander Graham Bell, a Scotsman, invented the telephone. The year 1880 brought Thomas Edison and the invention of the light bulb. B. B. graduated into a new world.

After leaving the island, B. B. stayed in touch with the school and maintained a subscription to the *Beacon*. In 1888, Charles H. Bradley

Chapter 1

became superintendent, and on February 19, 1898, B. B. wrote a letter to Mr. Bradley. The letterhead was very impressive and advertised his services as "Soloist for concerts, church and all first class entertainment." In the letterhead photo, Bertrand B. Keyes looks grand in his tuxedo and white bow tie, holding his cornet (figure 4).

In his letter he says,

> *Having traveled around the country from one location to the other also North and South, I still cherish the same kind of remembrances of the old school as though it was but yesterday that I left its protecting arms…In this time I had an opportunity of playing a month at the world's fair at Chicago and at the opening of the next year at the mid-winter fair…In my travels around the country I quite frequently ran across boys from the school and we talk over old school days.*

That February, B. B. traveled on a ship bound to London, England, with the Salem Cadet Band. The band proved to be popular, and all seats were sold out wherever they played. In the same letter to Bradley, B. B. wrote, "The band [is] the finest and greatly in demand."

In 1887, B. B. had married Amelia Philbrick in Boston. Amelia had a twin sister Amanda, who would later live with them (figure 5). Mabel Keyes was born to Bertrand and Amelia on July 22, 1893, in Chicago, during the Exposition (figure 6). That same day Katherine Lee Bates wrote "America the Beautiful." It was full speed ahead, America.

Chapter 2

The Pan-American Exposition Disaster
1901

The same year that B. B. sailed to London, the US battleship *Maine* was blown up and Spain was held responsible. The US declared war on Spain, and newspapers had a field day. Journalists William Randolph Hearst and Joseph Pulitzer, both brilliant, powerful writers, publicized the war widely. In a year, Spain was defeated. The United States won a decisive victory and rose in the hierarchy of world powers.

In the fall of 1901, the Pan-American Exposition, a world's fair, was held in Buffalo, New York (figure 7). B. B. Keyes was a solo virtuoso in the Salem Cadet Band, and he travelled with the band to the exposition. Mabel Keyes, eight years old, stayed home with her mother in Lynn, Massachusetts. It was September and Mabel had to go to school. She was probably disappointed at not being with her father.

B. B. played the cornet in two cadet bands: the Salem (Massachusetts) and the Elgin (Illinois). Cadet bands were connected with a military unit but played for many non-military events including dances ("assemblies") and public holidays. All world fairs and expositions included concerts by many cadet bands. The highly acclaimed Salem Cadet Band was directed for sixty-three years by Jean Missud, a native of France, who died in 1941 ("Jean Missud," Wikipedia; McAllister n.d.).

Chapter 2

At the exposition on Friday, September 6, President McKinley was meeting and greeting the people. He was highly popular during the Spanish-American War. B. B. had a rehearsal that day in the Temple of Music, surrounded by large palm trees. He was excited to meet McKinley. The weather was ideal: mild with a cloudless sky.

McKinley had a pleasant personality. He shook hands with many thousands of ordinary people. But McKinley favored the privileged barons of industry: big oil, steel and railroads. Andrew Carnegie and John D. Rockefeller kept business going and growing.

Large crowds filed into the Temple of Music. B. B. Keyes was in line when the unthinkable happened. At exactly four o'clock, a bullet grazed McKinley, then the second shot from a concealed revolver hit his stomach. The anarchist, Leon Czolgosz, a deranged assassin, had fired the two shots. He was immediately overpowered by the police. McKinley cried, "Go easy on him, boys."

The bullet lodged deep in McKinley's abdomen, and the doctors could not locate it after operating for over an hour. Infection set in. There were then no antibiotics with which to treat the infection. The newspapers downplayed the seriousness of the president's condition. Meanwhile the Salem Cadet Band continued to play under the direction of Jean Missud. They played "The Song of Victory" among other upbeat, patriotic pieces.

While the band played, the president took a turn for the worse. The newspapers reported the shocking details. On September 14, President McKinley died of gangrene. His assassin was later tried and executed. Theodore Roosevelt, who was a progressive Republican, became president of the United States.

Chapter 3

Wedding and Warfare
1907–1916

In the early twentieth century, color postcards were a popular means of communication, especially when travelling or on vacation. The Keyes family and friends exchanged many postcards and Mabel saved them all. B. B. Keyes travelled extensively with the two cadet bands and sent many postcards to his wife and daughter. During the summer of 1907, he wrote postcards from concert venues in Maine. July 23, a postcard from South Freeport asks fourteen-year-old Mabel, "Do you ever go bathing?" A postcard from Rowe's Point, says, "They are going to have a band here for the next two Sundays. We get through playing here on Labor Day and we go to Mere Point for three weeks." From Waterville on May 20, 1911, B. B. wrote his family, "Hope you are having a good time. Will be glad to get back again." Mabel and her friends exchanged postcards about their summer vacations and whether or not they were practicing their music (figure 8).

Mabel was fascinated by the theatre and water-color painting. Amelia was talented at oil painting but was probably not fond of actors as she referred to them as "the theatre crowd." She considered the theatre business to be low-class and sleazy. In contrast, Mabel loved the theatre and compiled an album of photos of theatre stars, actors, and actresses. B. B. Keyes was close to his daughter. As a young girl, Mabel always called him "Poppa," but called Amelia "Mother," a more formal title.

B. B. had encouraged her to take up the violin, and Mabel was talented and already doing very well. At the age of sixteen, she accompanied

Chapter 3

students in recitals. It is highly likely that such a young and very talented violinist would have attended the Boston Conservatory of Music. Unfortunately, the Conservatory records for the years she would have been a student there are incomplete or were destroyed in a fire. Eventually, however, she would become a professional musician like her father.

In 1915, Mabel was twenty-two years old. She was "recognized as one of the finest violinists east of New York." The cover of the December 1915 magazine of the Lonergan Players displayed her photo with her violin. Inside was a laudatory article about her (figure 9). The Lonergan Players were founded and directed by Lester Lonergan, born in Ireland in 1893, a successful actor, director and playwright.

War was on the horizon that year. Germany published in their newspapers in large print, "Notice! Travelers intending to embark on Atlantic voyages are reminded that the state of war [exists]…Vessels flying the flag of Great Britain are liable to be attacked in those waters, and travelers sailing in the war zone do so at their own risk." On May 1, a German submarine torpedoed the American tanker *Gulf Light* (Berg 2013, 354).

Later that year, the luxury ship *Lusitania* was sunk in the Irish Sea by the Germans. Mabel was indignant and turned against the "Huns." George V changed his royal name from Saxe Coburg-Gotha to the British name Windsor (Coetzee 1995, 32).

The young Mabel Keyes believed in a democratic and civilized America. She was for rigorous competition, but also for fair play; she played by the rules. Mabel favored underdogs both black and white, men and women. She was conservative about "free market" economics but liberal about justice for blacks. Mabel hated racism and injustice.

Wilson had created the system of segregation in schools and on public transportation. The NAACP loudly objected to the government's policies, saying that they "set the colored people apart." Wilson had not intended such a result, as he "did not equate segregation with subjugation" (Berg 2013, 309).

In November 1916, there was a second-term presidential election. Charles Evans Hughes, a former Supreme Court judge, was running against

Wilson. Mabel favored Hughes because she did not trust Wilson, who was a Southerner. She felt that Wilson was probably a racist. For three days after the election, Mabel thought that Hughes had won. As a woman, Mabel could not vote until 1920.

In Europe fighting was fierce, particularly in France and Belgium. The battlefield trenches of the Somme and Flanders were deep in rain and mud. There were barbed wire, tear gas, and mustard gas; the dead lay everywhere. Above in the skies, the famous German hero, the "Red Baron," Count Manfred von Richthofen, fought in his red biplane, wearing his helmet and goggles with his red scarf flying in the open air. Thousands of soldiers died in battles in North Africa, at Gallipoli, and in many other places all over the globe.

Under the firm hand of President Wilson, the US remained neutral until April 6, 1917, when the US Congress declared war on Germany. That year, imperial Germany had declared a new policy of "unrestricted submarine warfare" and had sunk several American ships. "The time of patience has passed," wrote President Wilson; "The world must be safe for democracy."

During the Great War, Mabel was very patriotic and became interested in international affairs. Her world was constantly evolving. She was reading mostly non-fiction and listening to radio news to learn about the world. She was a highly intelligent person. She already had compassion for the African-Americans. However, in her journals she did not mention the increasing violence of the Ku Klux Klan, founded in 1915. Klan members were also active in the northern states, such as Vermont in 1919, when they joined a public parade. Their uncivilized and violent racism became a legal institution.

Mabel pursued her promising career as a professional musician. She played in an all-women orchestra at theatres in Lynn and Quincy and gave private violin lessons (figure 10). Billy DeWolfe was forty-one years old and a famous comedian of vaudeville. It is possible that the two met during their theatrical work and admired each other's professional expertise. In addition, Mabel was an auburn-haired beauty. Despite the almost twenty-years' difference in their ages, they agreed to marry the next year.

Chapter 3

In her journal of May 3, 1916, Mabel wrote, "I took the train to Boston in the AM after filing my marriage intentions at City Hall. Billy filed his in Springfield." Billy was acting in plays at the Poli's Theatre built there in 1904, one of the many theatres built by S. Z. Poli.

On May 8, Mabel's journal entry begins, "My wedding day." In the morning she walked downtown and shopped, then "took the 12:10 Boston car" to South Station, then the two o'clock train to Springfield, arriving about 4:30 p.m. She met Billy at the Poli's Theatre, where he was playing, and friends took them to a reverend where "Billy and I were married about 6 o'clock." He was dressed in his costume for the performance that evening, which Mabel attended. "The co. gave Billy and I [sic] an electric chafing dish, spoon and fork after the performance," she wrote. No notes about wedding dress, the one bridesmaid, flowers, reception—the usual concerns of a young bride.

During the following couple weeks, the newlyweds enjoyed Springfield, often dining at the Observatory Restaurant, set high above the city and affording a "wonderful view."

Chapter 4

Marriage and Two Careers
1916–1919

Their marriage was really a "modern" one in that after a couple of weeks' "honeymoon" in Springfield, they separated to pursue their own careers. They met in hotels in Springfield, Boston, and New Haven—wherever Billy was working—and in a rented New York apartment when Billy was a theatre manager there. Mabel remained primarily in Lynn with her parents, although in the spring of 1919, Mabel and Billy were living temporarily in Boston. They bought their first home in 1920 in Merrymount, a suburb of Quincy, where they finally lived together when not on the road with their careers. They exchanged frequent postcards during their separations (figure 11).

June 14, a day after returning home to Lynn from her wedding in Springfield, Mabel left by train for Waterville, Maine, to play in a small orchestra at the Silver Street Theatre, accompanying the silent films shown there. She boarded with Hattie, also a member of the Auditorium ("Audi") Theatre orchestra in Lynn, and they both played for the Maine theatre. The first night the film was *The Girl of Yesterday*, starring Mary Pickford. She thought John Barrymore was a "dandy comedian." It was a cold, rainy month in Waterville.

Playing for the silent films was hard work. Mabel notes, "I was very tired tonight. They ran 2 whole shows so we didn't get out until 10:40 o'clock." Later she notes that playing for the horseback chases in westerns was especially exhausting. She remembers when Tom Mix came onstage in the Audi with his horse!

Chapter 4

It wasn't all work, however. With Hattie she toured the cotton and paper mills, went to see a log jam on the Kennebec River, and picked violets in the woods. At the woolen mills in Oakland, she bought material for a skirt. She and Hattie often walked to the Opera House to see the current performance. They usually walked everywhere, and she notes when they get a ride in an "auto" or "machine."

The season at the Silver Street Theatre closed on June 24. "I was so glad," she writes, "as I am anxious to get home." No mention of Billy in her journal while in Maine. On June 25, she took the "N.G. [narrow gauge] train" to Boston and then the "4:45 Pullman to Springfield. Hubby met me at the train." Together again for the first time since their wedding. The next evening, she watches the performance of *Sinners*. "Hubby plays Willie Morgan." Billy is busy with rehearsals, often late at night, and matinee and evening performances at the Poli's Theatre. A new play every week. Mabel takes advantage of her free time to walk, shop, and sew, practices a little, as well as attends Billy's evening shows in his dressing room or in the audience.

One night after midnight, they see a rat in their hotel room and move to another room. It's quite hot in Springfield now and "Billy isn't feeling well. I guess it is the heat." Billy has several dental appointments and will continue to have dental problems.

She notes that July 22 is "my 23rd birthday…I did a lot of…shopping." Her purchases included glasses for Billy, who was forty-three. Mabel stayed in Springfield until August 26, when she returned to Lynn and her parents. She continued her work in the all-women orchestra at the Audi, playing for silent pictures, and gave private violin lessons. She often attended performances and movies and commented on them in her journal. She was always busy, trimming her hats and making or altering her clothes, and visiting Betty, Billy's sister, in Boston.

Her father, B. B., was also busy. Her journal records that, "Dad has been with the Salem Band in Barnstable for 3 days playing for the Fair," and that he plays at the Relay House in Nahant. He plays somewhere just about every day. She makes and sends two shirts to Billy.

In 1917, the Audi season ended on May 26. That summer, Mabel played with "the girls" at the Relay House in Nahant, a popular summer resort on two islands connected to Lynn by a narrow spit of land. On May 31, she met six of what must have been a core group of nine or ten women musicians. They were in Winthrop rehearsing for Nahant. During the season, she often took the jitney, a small bus, to and from Nahant.

Her group played afternoon and evening performances for the vacationers and summer residents. Their day often didn't end until 10:30 at night. That June also was cold and rainy. Sometimes high winds and rain would cancel a performance. In her journal of Sunday, July 8, she writes, "I don't like Sundays at Nahant. In fact, I dislike the place all the time. Would much rather be with my hubby."

Mabel frequently would meet Billy in Boston, sometimes for overnight at the Savoy Hotel. All her traveling was done on public transportation. Sunday, July 22, is noted as her twenty-fourth birthday, and she has "a very bad head cold."

On October 16, 1917, Mabel, carrying two violins, along with four or five other women musicians, set off in a train headed south from Boston to join a tour of military bases by the Mikado Opera Co. The women stopped overnight in New York City, Mabel in order to meet "Hubby," who was manager of the large Hoyt's circuit theatres in the city. The next morning Billy and Mabel said goodbye until December 5, when Mabel would return from the train tour.

The troupe traveled by train south through Tennessee, to Chattanooga, New Orleans, west through Texas, and eventually north to Grand Rapids, Michigan, before returning to New York City. Letters and telegrams from Billy arrived for her daily, and in her journal, Mabel spoke frequently of missing "Hubby."

In her journal, Mabel described each day of the tour: Chattanooga, Tennessee, October 16: "The boys seemed to enjoy the performance. A big crowd." The weather in the south was colder than she had expected. At Camp Oglethorpe, Georgia, in mid-October, Mabel wrote, "I really

Chapter 4

froze coming home, but there was a good crowd at the performance." New Orleans, October 29: "An awful change in temperature."

Mabel described playing the violin with difficulty because it was freezing in the canvas tent—about 35° F. She noted the New Orleans delta and its marshes and small shacks that the train passed. "I registered in the Bazos Hotel…I am homesick the first day," Mabel wrote.

Texas, November 5: At Camp Logan, Mabel played excerpts from *The Mikado* at dinner for many men and women. She was apparently impressed with Camp Logan. "I spent most of the day in the observation car watching the very picturesque scenery…[I] wrote a letter to Billy and checked out of the hotel."

Meanwhile, on the eastern front of the Great War, the retreat of the Russian soldiers became a rout. The tsar abdicated in November of 1917. On the train, Mabel watched the wind blow away the smoke and steam from the locomotive. The date was November 11, 1917, exactly a year before Germany would surrender.

Later in November she wrote, "The concert was at night in a tent, and the electric lights were not working. We played most of the performance by candlelight." In San Antonio, Texas, she had time to visit the Alamo. November 29, Grand Rapids, Michigan: "[I] had a dandy Thanksgiving dinner at the Arcade Restaurant. At 5:45 I played in a fine auditorium to a very large, appreciative audience."

In early December, Billy and Mabel reunited in New York City and stayed at the St. Regis Hotel, where they had dinner after Mabel had "a nice, hot bath." Later she wrote, "My raccoon coat came."

During her train tour of military bases in 1917, Mabel had been in Kansas City. In January of the following year, a Spanish flu epidemic broke out in that city. It was "an unusual and deadly pandemic…Most influenza outbreaks disproportionately kill juvenile, elderly, or already weakened patients" ("1918 Flu Pandemic," Wikipedia). Mabel and her two children, born in 1918 and 1920, years of the epidemic, were fortunate to be spared.

Final Curtain

During the winter of 1918, Mabel visited many military hospitals. Several young soldiers had pneumonia and the dreaded tuberculosis. Antibiotics were not yet invented. She accomplished a lot: caring, advising, supporting, and playing her violin for the soldiers. During the Great War, Mabel matured into a courageous, independent woman.

After the war ended, B. B. Keyes retired from his musical career. Amelia had never liked the cold winters of the East Coast. In the fall of 1919, they took the Overland Limited to Los Angeles. Traveling across Wyoming, Amelia wrote to Mabel in pencil describing their trip. Her spelling and grammar are not perfect but her descriptions are lively. She talks at length about the good and copious food and its cost in the dining car.

A family in their car includes three daughters who "all do a good deal of powdering mother," and Amelia wonders if she should not have thrown away her own face powder before leaving. In Chicago, there was some time between trains and Amelia notes, "quite a number of changes since we were there." She is referring to 1893, twenty-six years before, when she and B. B. were in Chicago for the Columbian Exposition and Mabel was born. "But the people," she writes, "are in just the same rush as ever." She is thoroughly enjoying the trip.

Four days later, Amelia writes another letter, in pen, from the one-room apartment they rented upon arrival in Los Angeles. She is pleased with and describes at length the amenities of this furnished studio apartment. They look for their friends, Frank and Ethel, and finally find them at their jobs. Frank and Ethel are surprised to see them.

Mabel will not see her father again before he dies in 1935. In 1941, Mabel herself travels by train to Los Angeles to care for her aging mother and her twin sister.

Chapter 5

Everybody Knows Billy
1874–1928

William Whitmore "Billy" DeWolfe was born on April Fool's Day 1874, in Boothbay, Maine. Ulysses Grant was president and automobiles would not be invented for another decade.

Billy was the sixth of seven children of Isiah (1834–1914) and Ellen MacDonald DeWolfe (1836–1899), originally from Nova Scotia (figure 12). There were five girls and two boys. Jenny was the oldest. Then came Robert, born 1860, who committed suicide in 1930. Eunice was third, and Laura fourth. Laura was born in 1865 and died in a carriage accident in 1895. Lizzie, who later became Elizabeth or Betty, was born in 1867. Billy followed in 1874, and Grace was the last, born in 1876 and died in 1963 (figure 13).

From an early age, Billy was interested in the theatre. He put on plays in a local barn and charged the neighborhood children nails and pennies for admission. This led to a long and successful career on the vaudeville stage, principally as a comedian. Billy did blackface, country rube routines, comic monologues, and clog and sand dancing. In 1898, he successfully tried out for the part of Hi Holler in the original production of *Way Down East*.

This long-running play kept him in one place for a season, but he traveled all over the US and played on many stages. He had a national following but was particularly well known in New England. When the nineteenth century ended, Billy was still acting at twenty-six years of age (figure 14).

In 1915, he was in a stock company in Lynn when he met a beautiful violinist named Mabel Keyes, who played in the Auditorium Theatre's all-women orchestra. He was only a few blocks away at the Lindsay-Morison Playhouse. Mabel was nothing like the women Billy had known in theatre life. After every performance, she returned home to her cooking and sewing.

In the spring of 1916, they were married. On September 5, 1918, their first child, (Ellen) Barbara, was born in Boston (figure 15). That same year, Billy retired from the stage and began his career as a theatre manager. He now had a family to support, was probably tired of traveling, and wanted to spend more time at home. He managed theatres in New York City before taking over the management for Fred Murphy in Quincy of two combination theatres (vaudeville show and a movie), the Quincy and the Strand, and a movie house, the Alhambra.

A second daughter, Eunice Elizabeth, was born on April 26, 1920 (figure 16). Eunice proved to be talented with the violin and an artist, too. The family moved to a house on Chickatabot Road in the Quincy suburb of Merrymount. The house was located across the bay.

Quincy was and is a beautiful seaside city. It has several districts: Squantum, Norfolk Downs, Merrymount, Wollaston, West Quincy, South Quincy, Adams Shore, Braintree; and the suburbs, Fore River and Hough's Neck. Around the city center were beaches, marshes, and granite quarries (figure17).

Although no longer active on the stage, Billy was an important and influential part of the Quincy theatre scene. He was a brilliant conversationalist and much sought after by hostesses. The people of Quincy were sure they had a celebrity in their midst. He dressed the part: flannel suits, shiny gold watch chain and fob, and spats—always spats (figure 18).

He encouraged young actors, and a recommendation from him counted for a lot. Around 1924, Billy Andrew Jones was a young usher as well as an excellent dancer, comedian, and contortionist. The teenager had potential and Billy DeWolfe supported him. "Billy Jones is a golfer," Billy laughed, "Take my name." Jones changed his name and became Billy De Wolfe, a future vaudeville, TV, and movie star. (He changed the last name to two words.) Among friends and family, he was Billy De Wolfe, Jr.

Chapter 5

Biographies of Billy, Jr., such as in the encyclopedia *Vaudeville Old and New*, do not mention DeWolfe at all or say that Bill "appropriated the theatre manager's name" (Cullen 2007, 309). All his life, young Billy was grateful to Billy DeWolfe for giving him his name. Even after Billy's death, young Billy stayed in close touch with Mabel and the girls. He considered himself a member of the family.

Mabel and Billy were unique and modern partners in the entertainment world. Mabel created the all-women orchestra, the Wolverines, in 1920. Mabel was excellent at advertising the orchestra, and for four years the Wolverines were highly popular in the Quincy region. Billy and Mabel were at the top of their game (figure 19).

One day in 1924, the Wolverines are ready for the rehearsal of the evening program. The star of the evening, a chauvinistic comedian, refuses to go onstage with the women. Billy's face reddens, "What do you mean this show can't go on?" The star is the young Milton Berle. Mabel is offended. Billy raises his voice in anger. "And what about THEM?" asks Billy, pointing to the Wolverines. Billy is not intimidated by Milton Berle. "You go on with them, or you don't go on at all!" Berle went onstage.

Billy DeWolfe was a prosperous theatre manager and Mabel directed her own band. In 1926, Mabel was thirty-three and Billy was fifty-two. For Mabel, her career was at its height. Billy was at home, settled, and locally famous, but he was stressed and not well. He gained weight—about thirty pounds. No one warned him of the hidden danger.

At that time, the movie business was experimenting with sound. Two years later, the first full-length talking picture appeared, *The Jazz Singer*, starring Al Jolson.

They both continued their successful careers separately and together until late December 1926, when Billy became ill, was hospitalized, and finally suffered a massive stroke at the age of fifty-two.

Billy's speech was slurred. He was partially paralyzed and used a cane to walk. He spent lots of money going to the doctors, but rehabilitation was in its infancy. Billy apparently gave up. He was impatient, irritable, and pessimistic. Years later, his eldest daughter Barbara remembers him saying angrily, "I'm trying, dammit!" Barbara never forgot it (figure 20).

During his illness and stroke, many cards and letters arrived from his colleagues in the theatre business and from his admirers (figure 21). That Christmas a tree stood in the Merrymount home, adorned with over two hundred cards and letters to Billy (figure 22). Billy De Wolfe, Jr., sent a telegram from Nebraska where he was on stage:

> *Just heard that you are at home. Am so glad. Am sure you will be well and strong again real soon. Will write you a very long letter in a few days and tell all the news. Wishing you and Mrs. DeWolfe a very Merry Christmas and a Happy New Year. Am very thankful that you are home for Christmas. Billy.*

Eight-year-old daughter Barbara wrote a letter neatly in pencil:

> *Dear Mother and Father, I wish you the happiest Christmas you have ever had. May the Christ child bring you many blessings and success in the coming year. Your loving daughter, Barbara DeWolfe.*

At Barbara's sensitive age, she was serious and worried about her father's stroke.

Chapter 6

Testimonial Dinners and the Great Depression
1928–1931

In the following years before his death, at least three testimonial dinners and performances were held honoring Billy (figure 23).

The first dinner was in 1928. That spring Charles Augustus Lindbergh, an obscure US Mail pilot, flew the *Spirit of St. Louis* monoplane across the Atlantic in thirty-three hours. Lindbergh, a handsome twenty-five-year-old man, became an instant success around the globe ("Charles Lindbergh," Wikipedia).

America was confident, brave and proud. In contrast, Billy was helpless. "ACTOR LAUDS DEWOLFE," wrote the *Quincy Patriot Ledger,* announcing the first of the dinners and performances. The monster testimonial night in the Quincy Strand theatre was "nearly a sellout." Andrew "Bossy" Gillis, known far and wide as the mayor of Newburyport, was the master of ceremonies. An unexpected part of the entertainment was the appearance of actress Georgette Cohan, daughter of George M. Cohan, even though she was under a union contract at the time. George was a very successful playwright, actor, and producer of musicals; his daughter was equally successful onstage.

After three years of convalescence, Billy was not getting better. He was "one of the most widely known and best beloved theatrical men in the country," wrote the *Ledger*. Quincy Mayor Thomas J. McGrath, a longtime friend, was worried about Billy and attended the testimonial dinners.

One year later, the nationally famous comedian Fred Allen counted himself as a friend of Billy's. "FRED ALLEN TO HEAD BILL AT DEWOLFE TESTIMONIAL" (*Quincy Patriot Ledger*). The second testimonial, on Washington's birthday in 1929, featured Fred Allen as MC. "Fred Allen, nature's gift to an audience and star of the 'Little Show' in Boston will lead the bill at the midnight show at the Strand theatre" continued the article. The entertainment included "Dr." Rockwell, the star of the Greenwich Village Follies.

The last of the testimonial dinners was in 1931. The Boston sports writer, Bill Cunningham, was part of the entertainment. Fred B. Murphy, owner of the theatre, spoke briefly to thank all those who had contributed to the dinners and following performances. The picture part of the program was a newsreel and a comedy. Again, it was a sellout.

Three years earlier, during the "Roaring 20s," people were spending lots of money carelessly. There was an atmosphere of plenty. During the years of the testimonial dinners, catastrophe struck the US: in October 1929, the stock market crashed and began the Great Depression. By 1931, 25% of Americans were unemployed. The country's economy was a disaster, which led to widespread panic.

Mabel and her daughters—Barbara, twelve, and Eunice, ten—were worried about the Depression and about Billy's chronic illness. Mabel was still working hard with the Wolverines and aggressively advertising in the newspapers.

Already in 1928, Mabel had had a big advertisement in the *Ledger* for three days:

NOW SHOWING – "THE BIG PARADE"
EXTRA! ADDED!
MABEL DEWOLFE
and Her Hollywood Broadcasting Carleton Troubadours.

(The Hollywood Broadcasting Carleton Troubadours was another of the bands she led.) She was courageous and aggressive about advertising. A publicity photo, probably from the early 1930s, shows a lovely young

Chapter 6

violinist. A December 1930 newspaper article praises her as a professional female violinist (figures 24 and 25).

Mabel also wrote to fellow musicians for advice and help. Their responses were not hopeful and often described the gloomy outlook for musicians looking for work. Caroline Nichols headed her own group, The Clarion Trumpeters. In response to a letter from Mabel, she wrote that the "music business is pretty well 'shot'" and advises her to go into teaching (figures 26 and 27).

While Billy was incapacitated at home, Mabel had a full schedule playing for vaudeville and in the orchestra for the Auditorium Theatre as well as in other theatres. She often worked long days. It is possible that family members, such as Aunt Georgie, Amelia's sister, cared for Billy while Mabel worked.

Chapter 7

Strange Interlude (1929) and *Lord of the Flies* (1954)

O'Neill's play premiered in January 1928 at Broadway's John Golden Theatre in New York City. Critics lauded and condemned it; the latter as a "spectacle of immorality and advocacy of atheism, of domestic infidelity and the destruction of unborn human life," as the mayor of Boston said on banning a long-planned production in his city (Dowling 2014, 345).

Mayor Thomas McGrath of Quincy offered his city. "*Strange Interlude* by Eugene O'Neill opened at the Quincy Theatre on Monday, September 30, 1929," wrote Mabel in her "Compositions" book and pasted the program into it. The play closed Saturday, October 26, 1929, after a very successful run.

The play ran for five-and-a-half hours with a break for dinner at nearby restaurants. A popular one was owned by Howard Deering Johnson, who went on to build the largest hotel and restaurant chain in the country (Dowling 2014, 346).

Mabel did not go to the play, perhaps because of its controversial subject matter, but she was interested in and curious about it. Also pasted into her "Compositions" book was the commentary from the *Quincy Patriot Ledger*, "Farewell to Quincy" (figure 28). The journalist wrote,

> *After a run of four weeks, the play will pursue its sinister course to Springfield…Mayor McGrath said the restauranteurs were sitting pretty, and a good time was had by all.*

Chapter 7

Strange Interlude and *Lord of the Flies*, the novel by William Golding, have a similar theme: civilization versus savagery—and savagery triumphs. *Lord of the Flies* was published twenty-six years after *Strange Interlude*, and both won the Pulitzer Prize.

In *Strange Interlude* a principal character is Professor Marsden, "a dreamy self-analyst" and "physically weak," similar to Piggy in *Lord of the Flies*. Piggy loves books, as does the professor, whose library is lined with them. Books are the symbol of rational, civilized values in the play and the novel.

A decaying pig's head, the "Lord of the Flies," is a symbol of the evil Beelzebub and the chaos into which the boys descend. Piggy, a chubby boy with thick glasses, is rational and brainy and fond of reading. At the beginning of the novel, Piggy is a leader, but he is threatened by the surrounding jungle: "All around [Piggy] the scars smashed into the jungle which was a bath of heat." Piggy says, "I can't hardly move with all these creeper things," referring to the tangled, twisted plants. "There was that pilot," says Piggy. The "pilot" symbolizes authority and order.

Ralph, another of the boys, controls the conch, a symbol of authority. Ralph is physically strong; he seeks compromise between the civilized and uncivilized, the rational and the irrational, but still is a leader. Jack is a hunter, a fierce, violent, savage figure, emotionally uncontrolled with sexual energy.

Jack turns Piggy into a helpless, weak child with broken glasses. Eventually, Piggy is killed and everything turns into chaos. Ralph loses the battle for leadership to Jack. At the end of the novel, Ralph's tears "begin to flow and sobs shook him...Ralph wept for the end of innocence."

In a similar way, dark, sexual Nina Leeds shows that Professor Marsden is weak and ineffectual. Again chaos triumphs—a tragedy for civilization.

Civilization was "challenged" by World War II, according to FDR, because Hitler was a deranged and violent person who destroyed millions of people. During the chaos of the war, 250 million people perished.

For Mabel, society meant a civilized life, but war was a reality. Indeed, life is a jungle. The 1915 poem, "The Tide Will Turn" by Agnes Carr, expresses adversity and the survival of the fittest. Mabel clipped it out of the *Boston Traveller* in 1955, three years before her death.

The ocean dashes on the shore,
And then retreats with gesture wide;
And every day with kingly roar,
It comes and goes, the tide.

Adversity may come to you,
The tide of life run fierce and high;
But hold to this thought, staunchly true,
The tide will turn, stand by!

Chapter 8

After Billy
1932–1936

DEATH RINGS DOWN CURTAIN FOR DEWOLFE
—Front page, *Quincy Patriot Ledger*, September 23, 1932

Billy was fifty-nine years old when he died on September 23, 1932. Mabel and their two daughters were by his bedside in Merrymount. "Oh, Billy!" Mabel said. As was the custom in Merrymount, the coffin was in the dining room for three days of visitation and mourning.

Three newspapers—the *Quincy Patriot Ledger*, the *Boston Globe*, and the *Boston Herald Traveller*—covered DeWolfe's famous acting career (figure 29). Wrote one journalist in the *Ledger*:

> *'Bill' DeWolfe fulfilled the best traditions of the theatre. Because of his many years of experience, he was acknowledged to be an outstanding showman.*

While Mabel, a thirty-nine-year-old widow, was in mourning, she also continued looking for musical jobs. Lots of people were unemployed in the 1930s, but Mabel was aggressive and determined to work. She saved the many letters of sympathy for Billy's illness and of condolence on his death that she received. This letter is dated December 4, 1930, on the stationery of the Hotel Wolverine:

Dear Mabel, well, it has been some time since I have written, but I think of Billy very often, and I wonder how he is getting on…Hundreds of men are out of work…A terrible condition and I don't know where it is all going to end.

A letter from Edward White, a colleague in the theatre, said, "I am with George Cohan—playing the Tavern again. [I] may get around Boston again later in the Season. Lots of actors [are] out of work here—lucky to have a job. Drop me a line and let me know how Billy is."

Mabel wrote gracious letters introducing herself to potential employers. In those days, it was quite unusual for women—and especially a single woman—to be a professional violinist. She asked friends and colleagues for letters of recommendation for herself and the Wolverines. She established the DeWolfe Studio and gave lessons. Shortly after Billy's death she created the Beralde Trio (the final *e* is pronounced.) It was made up of Hildegard Berthold, cello; Agnes Allen, piano; and Mabel DeWolfe, violin. The name came from those of the three players. The trio was very popular and played for many events and regularly on WBZ, a Quincy radio station.

Mabel's parents, B. B. and Amelia Keyes, had moved to Los Angeles in 1919 when her father retired from his musical career. He was very proud of his daughter's achievements and especially of the Beralde Trio. Shortly before his death from stomach cancer in October of 1935, he wrote her a last letter:

Dear Mabel,

Well, it doesn't seem as if I am 71, the way I feel. Of course, I have some aches and pains. I must thank you for your kind remembrance of [my birthday] and I know that you still think about your dad…[I] am much better…I was very glad to hear of your good luck in getting some work…I was delighted to receive Barbara's picture. By the way, I think I have a little music which I brought with me among

Chapter 8

other things. If you want it, you are welcome to it.... Well, it is time for me to be on my way so with love and best wishes to you and Barbara and Eunice.

I remain your old dad,
B. B. Keyes

During the years of raising her daughters, Mabel earned money by playing in many different settings and for many different organizations. Aunt Georgie often cared for the girls. Mabel would play solo, with the trio, with the Wolverines, and with other variations of musical groups. Vaudeville theatres were a principal setting, such as the Auditorium in Lynn and the theatres in Quincy. Many churches and organizations frequently employed her. One was the Staley College of the Spoken Word in Brookline, Massachusetts. John F. Kennedy attended Staley College before leaving for the navy. Among other eminent Staley graduates are two former Boston mayors, James Michael Curley and Maurice Tobin.

Among the churches who employed her and the trio was the Bethany Congregational Church, a large, impressive church in the center of Quincy. In addition to church services, the church sponsored a theatre group called The Bethany Players. For the sacred holidays, the players put on theatrical performances, with music provided by the Beralde Trio.

Mabel also earned money outside of her musical career. For a short time, she sold girdles and white gloves, both in style at that time, and also worked as a real estate agent, principally for rental properties. All of her earnings now went into the bank. This contrasted starkly with the lavish spending of the 1920s, when she and Billy were at the height of their careers.

Meanwhile her two daughters, Barbara and Eunice, graduated from Quincy High School. Barbara attended Bridgewater State College and graduated with a teaching degree in 1939. Eunice attended the Massachusetts College of Art but did not get a degree.

Chapter 9

The Pre-war Years
1936–1941

In 1936, four years after Billy's death, storm clouds were brewing. Mabel always bought the *Quincy Patriot Ledger* and the *Boston Globe* to read about world events and listened to the news on the radio. In her journals she noted key world events but rarely, if ever, expressed opinions about them.

On the back pages of the *Quincy Patriot Ledger* and the *Boston Globe*, Mabel read about Spain's troubles. Gibraltar, in Spain, is strategically located at the entrance to the Mediterranean Sea, fifteen miles across the water from North Africa. During the Napoleonic Wars in the early 1800s, Spain lost Gibraltar to England. In the late 1800s, Spain lost many of its Latin American colonies, except the island of Cuba, ninety miles from the tip of Florida.

The summer of 1936, the Olympics opened in Nazi Germany; simultaneously Spain's fragile government deteriorated and the Spanish Civil War began. In 1939, Generalissimo Franco's forces, with the support of Italy and Germany, won the struggle. Franco became dictator of Spain until his death in 1975.

At first, the Spanish Civil War was considered by the governments of the rest of the world, including the US, to be a purely local struggle. Many individuals, however, joined the Republican forces, seeing them as opposing the spread of fascism.

Mabel was concerned about maintaining the traditions of democracy. The Spanish elections made her concerned about the problems in that

Chapter 9

country. Her fears turned out to be justified since Adolf Hitler used the Spanish Civil War as proving ground for his Nazi Brown Shirts and German military power. (For more information, see the appendix.)

In 1937 the German dirigible *Hindenburg* burst into flames at Lakehurst, New Jersey. The four fins of the Hindenburg were marked with large black swastikas. Thirty-five people were killed, and the journalists photographed the dirigible in flames, so the carnage was seen in news reels.

In the US, a dispute raged over participation in the developing world war. The isolationists—among them, Charles Lindbergh—did not want the US to enter the war, and they had a slim majority in the government. A year later, in 1938, Germany turned aggressive. The propaganda minister Joseph Goebbels pursued aggressively his policy against the Jews. "Kristallnacht" (the Night of Broken Glass) was violent and savage. Lots of Jewish stores were broken into and the Jews were afraid.

After the end of the Spanish Civil War in the spring of 1939, King George VI and his wife, Queen Consort Elizabeth, came to the United States for the first time. The British Empire was at the height of its power. FDR went to Shangri-La (now Camp David) to greet the royal couple. On the menu were frankfurters. "I have never eaten hot dogs," said the king. Amid the distractions of the state visit, war with Europe was three months away.

That same year, the world's fair was held in New York City. Mabel DeWolfe could take only one vacation, and her daughters were also working. Eunice got a summer job with Hendrie's Ice Cream in Milton. Barbara taught first grade as an intern.

Mabel and her two daughters took their vacation to go to the fair. They marveled at the hundreds of exhibits they saw. The centerpiece of the fair was the Trylon and Perisphere. Among the exhibits was black-and-white closed-circuit television. President Herbert Hoover had been shown the "TV" in 1928. TV was expensive and experimental. Mabel and her daughters saw the "Electro Moto-man" robot, a moving walkway, color photography, fluorescent lamps, air conditioning, and a keyboard-speech-operated synthesizer. They saw virtually all of the myriads of attractions at the fair.

Final Curtain

The New York World's Fair ended in the fall of 1940. When Japan joined the Axis powers and attacked Pearl Harbor on December 7, 1941, the US made up its mind and joined the Allied powers.

Mabel's two daughters were growing up and becoming independent. Barbara was twenty-three and Eunice twenty-one. Mabel was fiercely loyal to her daughters. Eunice had abruptly dropped out of the Massachusetts College of Art. She had a boyfriend, Edwin Tappan, a divorced man of thirty-one—ten years older than she. Mabel was worried and unhappy. When Eunice was in high school, Mabel was also worried about her immaturity, emotionalism, and mediocre grades. Eunice was talented in music and art, but she did not apply herself.

In her journal of Thursday, March 27, 1941, Mabel wrote:

> *Eunice telephoned around 11:30 p.m. to tell us that she and Ed Tappan had just married. [I] don't know any particulars as yet…They are married in Rockland at the Justice of the Peace. Rosemary, his sister, and his brother stood up for them.*

Later Mabel wrote, "I miss Eunice." She was certainly unhappy about that news.

Edwin Elden Tappan was born in 1909 in New Hampshire. His education ended with the eighth grade. To make money, he worked as a car mechanic, a short order cook, and, during Prohibition, sold liquor illegally. Although he grew to be strong and wiry, he suffered from asthma and frequent bouts of pneumonia, especially as a child. Later he was plagued with back problems that prevented him from working.

Ed's reputation was checkered at best, and Mabel knew about his various "careers." Her daughter's new husband rented a house for them in Saugus, a half hour from Quincy. That same year, 1941, Mabel heard that her mother, now a widow, and her twin sister were both in ill health. She sold the Chickatabot Road house and took the train to California. She would not return until nine years had passed.

Chapter 10

Walking Alone
1941–1950

On the train from Boston to Los Angeles, Mabel, like her mother, wrote letters in pencil to her aunts and Barbara describing in detail her long trip on the El Capitan. She notes that the train of about twelve cars is pulled by a coal engine and three diesel engines. She found Ohio to be like New England, but "[I] rather liked the wide, vast plains of Kansas even though the wheat had been harvested. I could see the yellow stubble that was left." She was charmed by the scenery of the Southwest. She liked the meals in the dining car and gave their prices: breakfast 40–75 cents, luncheon 50–85 cents, and dinner 65 cents–$1.00.

Mabel talked with her fellow passengers and wrote, "I made up my mind that I wouldn't be accused of being a narrow Bostonian." The first day out of Boston, "a Wop plunked himself beside me and didn't move until we reached Utica. Was I glad when he changed seats, he and his garlic etc. sandwiches. No romance for me this trip."

In Chicago, friends from the theatre world picked her up, drove her around, and took her home for dinner, where she could take a shower. Billy, Jr. was playing in the city and they saw his name on a marquee. However, there wasn't time to catch his act before her train left at 5:45 p.m.

As the train neared Los Angeles, she wrote in a letter how "thrilled I am" to be in California, and then described some of the other occupants of her car. Although the train arrived on time in Los Angeles, Mabel's trunks were not aboard and would not arrive until the next day. Mabel took a taxi to the twin's house at 1126 W. 55th St. in Santa Monica, a suburb, arriving around 8:45 a.m. It was July 22, the day before her forty-eighth birthday.

In a later letter to Barbara, Mabel writes about meeting her mother after almost twenty-five years: "I wouldn't have known mother, she has changed so and she said she wouldn't have known me." The house was a duplex bungalow with Amelia's twin sister, Amanda, living on the other side. From childhood, the twins had been known as "Pink" (Amelia) and "Dime" (Amanda) after characters in a children's book. Their doctor, who made frequent visits, said the twins had high blood pressure and bad hearts. He wanted Mabel to get them out of the house more.

In the same letter, she says, "I shall be horribly homesick for a while." The nurse left the next day, after showing Mabel around the neighborhood a bit. Then Mabel took the twins for a walk. She ends the letter asking Barb to write often, as letters take a long time to arrive: "I shall long for letters from home."

In her California journals, Mabel does not record writing to or receiving many letters from Eunice. Her younger daughter's elopement disappointed and upset her, and there seemed to have been little communication between mother and daughter while Mabel was in California. Fortunately, relations were re-established when Mabel returned to the East.

In Santa Monica with her mother and aunt, Mabel wrote many letters because she missed Quincy. In her journal of August 9, 1941, she wrote, "[I] finally received a letter from Barb (bless her!)...[I] sent a letter to Edna May Oliver." Edna was ill and died that year before she could respond to two letters from Mabel. She was devastated by the news of Edna's untimely death at age fifty-nine. Edna was a well-known comedienne and a friend whom Mabel admired very much.

Her mother wasn't much company. Amelia was polite, formal, but distant, and chronically ailing. Her daughter was a servant to her "stomach problems." Mabel did not express her feelings in her journal. She was a private person who did not complain, even to herself.

In 1941, Los Angeles was intermittently foggy. The number of people and cars grew very fast. A new word entered the dictionary to name the

Chapter 10

combination of smoke and fog, "smog." This was very dangerous for older or weaker people. The elderly sisters did not like going outdoors when it was smoggy. Mabel commented in her journal: "It was hazy. I looked out over the city. [I] couldn't see far." About twenty years in the future, the climate would become oppressive.

Because the sisters did not go out much, Mabel walked around the city mostly alone. In her journal she described her many walks:

> *Then I walked downtown via Wilshire Boulevard…It took almost 2 hours…I rested in Lafayette Park for about five minutes. [I] saw the lovely Shakespearean Garden…[I] also walked through Westlake Park…[I] passed the Brown Derby.*

Walking became a habit:

> *September 5: Fog. Clearing around 10 AM. I walked up to 60th Street and mailed the letters to Eunice, Barbara and Elizabeth…Today is Barbara's 23rd birthday…[I] walked to 58th Street markets and did the shopping…I walked to 48th Street post office to mail letters. [I] stopped in the Library on my way back and got the card to fill out so I can get books. Mother had to sign it.*

She often walked to the public library to take out books. One was James Michener's *Hawaii*. Mabel was constantly reading, usually non-fiction, probably because she preferred reading in silence to making small talk with her mother. Amelia talked only of trivial niceties and pleasantries. It was a very different life from Mabel's East Coast life of music, theatre, and movies.

Mabel was always interested in global events, and she listened to the news on the radio. Every day, she listened to the *People's Platform* at 3 p.m. and the *Chicago Roundtable*. Mabel was concerned about political events involving Germany and Japan. She was an internationalist and a reader, and her philosophy was, "It's going to happen."

Summer turned to fall. "Mrs. Roosevelt spoke at 6 PM on the radio saying the US Navy will sink the Axis ships that interfere with areas vital for our defense," wrote Mabel in her journal.

Columbus Day, October 12, 1941: "Cloudy all day," wrote Mabel. That afternoon, "I walked up to Allen and Huck's and got frankfurts and ice cream after lunch." She heard on the radio about the men and women in the military.

November 9: "We three walked to the Harvard Playground to see the soldiers from San Luis Obispo…quite interesting sight—all the pup tents, trucks and military equipment."

On November 17, she wrote: "President Roosevelt signed the bill repealing the neutrality law."

December 7, 1941, a momentous day in history: "Japan began bombing Pearl Harbor…We heard the announcement while we were listening to 'Chicago Round Table'."

The next day, "President Roosevelt addressed Congress and declared war on Japan at 12:40 PM, EST [Eastern Standard Time]." Mabel wrote down exactly when the US joined the Second World War.

On Christmas day, Mabel wrote in her journal, "Peace on Earth, good will to men," a sentiment awkwardly out of place at the beginning of global warfare. Amelia, Amanda, and Mabel marked the holiday in an understated way with a small Christmas tree, "We listened to the radio and I read papers—a quiet day."

New Year's Day, 1941: "I walked to the post office and got stamps and mailed a letter to Barb." As usual, Mabel walked alone.

Chapter 11

Billy De Wolfe, Jr., and Hollywood

During Mabel's nine-year stay in California, Barbara often visited, and the two women traveled together, including to Hollywood where they visited Billy De Wolfe, Jr. There Mabel apparently met James Cagney because in her possessions is a large photo of him signed, "To Mabel K. DeWolfe, sincerely, James Cagney." On the back was written "August 13, 1942." Cagney starred in *Yankee Doodle Dandy*, directed by George M. Cohan. President Roosevelt enjoyed the film immensely, and it won five Academy Awards (figure 30).

Billy Andrew Jones was a native of Wollaston, part of Quincy, born in 1907. After the older Billy gave him his name, he went on to a successful career in vaudeville, films, and finally on TV. Quincy was very proud of him and Billy was proud of it (figure 31).

Billy became almost a member of the DeWolfe family and visited frequently. Family photos show Billy, Jr., visiting at the DeWolfe home in Merrymount. He and Barbara had immediately become fast friends (figures 32, 33 and 34).

Especially after the older Billy's death in 1932, Billy, Jr., visited Mabel and the girls whenever he could, wrote frequent postcards and letters, and sent telegrams. Many people who saw him perform assumed he was the son of Mabel and Billy. They wrote Mabel admiring letters about her husband and "son."

Billy first became famous for his comedy skits, performed mostly in nightclubs. In 1932 he sailed for Europe and would not return for five years. He was popular there and had many bookings. He first gave a four-week performance at the Café de Paris, then on to Glasgow, Edinburgh, and London. He had four command performances before the British royal family. He was better known in Europe than in his home country (figure 35).

On his return to America in 1937, he was booked solid and very happy. In his Christmas card to Mabel that year he describes his many performances, all of which were "hits." He concludes by saying, "So in staying away five years I have helped myself here in America." He served in the US Navy during World War II before returning to the stage and screen.

One of the first films he was in was *Dixie* in 1943. An August photo in the *Quincy Patriot Ledger* (pasted into one of Mabel's scrap books) shows him with co-stars Dorothy Lamour and Bing Crosby. The caption claims that Billy "really steals the show from such veteran performers as the beauteous Lamour and the one and only Bing" (figure 36). After *Dixie* came films such as *Perils of Pauline* and *Our Hearts Were Growing Up*, before he began work in the fall of 1946 on *Blue Skies*, which made him a star along with Fred Astaire, Bing Crosby, and Joan Caulfield.

The plot of *Blue Skies*, which is presented in a series of flashbacks with Astaire as the narrator, follows a familiar formula of Crosby beating out Astaire for the affections of a leading lady. Comedy was principally provided by Billy De Wolfe, playing Tony, the maître d' of a restaurant.

In the film, Billy presented his hilarious, twenty-minute monologue as Mrs. Phoebe Murgatroyd. With "her" prissy flowered green hat, she sat in the bar alone with two grocery bags—celery sticking out of one. The middle-aged lady, after protesting that she did not drink, ordered a 90-proof "Side-Kick" and suddenly got drunk. At the end, she exited tipsily and caused lots of laughter in the movie theatre. About ten years later, an April 11, 1955, cartoon of Billy De Wolfe with his flowered hat and spectacles was still a hit.

"Did you see *Life* magazine?" wrote Billy DeWolfe proudly to Mabel after the film's premiere. "It [*Blue Skies*] has been chosen as the Christmas

Chapter 11

attraction" (figure 37). The *Life* magazine article contained a photo of Billy with his trimmed moustache. Billy spent that Christmas in Quincy and a *Quincy Patriot Ledger* article announced that "Quincy Still First" with the actor. Again in 1953 another article headlines "Billy DeWolfe Works Quincy into his New Musical Revue" (figures 38 and 39).

In a postcard he wrote to Mabel, "I had hoped to get home for Memorial Day—but it just wasn't possible—I hope you are well, and let me hear from you often—all good wishes, Billy." (Billy De Wolfe liked dashes.)

During the filming of *Blue Skies*, Billy invited Mabel and Barbara to visit him on the set. Billy finished filming at noon, and Mabel and Barbara greeted him at his dressing room. Large black-and-white photos were taken of the three of them in front of his dressing room door. "It's been a long time," said the famous star. Indeed, Billy De Wolfe was moving up in the headlines (figure 40).

Towards the end of his career, Billy launched into TV. He was an old-maidish neighbor on the *Doris Day Show*, and a too fastidious radio station manager on *Good Morning, World*. He was the voice of the magician in the classic Christmas special, *Frosty the Snowman*. His last appearance was on tape after his death in Marlo Thomas's *Free to be You and Me*, a TV special (figure 41).

Billy was a heavy smoker and he died of lung cancer in March 1974 in California at the age of sixty-seven. Barbara DeWolfe attended the simple ceremony at the Mount Wollaston Baptist Church, where Billy was eulogized by many (figure 42). His ashes are buried in Hollywood and in the Mount Wollaston cemetery. His epitaph reads:

Billy De Wolfe
1907   1974
William A. Jones

Chapter 12

Barbara DeWolfe and the Bretton Woods Conference 1944

Mabel encouraged her daughters to take summer jobs to help with the family's finances. Barbara, who taught during the school year, always had a summer job. In 1935 she was an attendant at a children's hospital in Egypt, Massachusetts. Subsequent summers were spent first as a city playground instructor and then as a waitress in such establishments as the Holderness Inn, where she enjoyed the New Hampshire environment.

In the summer of 1944, while Mabel was in Los Angeles, Barbara got a job as waitress at the Mount Washington Hotel in Bretton Woods in the White Mountains of New Hampshire. The Mount Washington Hotel is a majestic, white building with a distinctive red roof at the base of Mount Washington. The grand hotel was finished in 1902. Next to the golf course stands a chapel with large stained glass windows designed by Tiffany. The mountains of New Hampshire were far away from the terrible fighting around the world. Germany and Japan were slowly losing the war (figure 43).

That summer, the hotel was the site of the historic United Nations Monetary and Financial Conference, which became known as the Bretton Woods Conference. Barbara DeWolfe was excited about meeting the VIPs coming to the conference from all over the world.

Chapter 12

At the historic, two-month conference, Lord Maynard Keynes, the famous British advisor and economist, officiated along with Secretary of the Treasury Henry Morgenthau, Secretary of State Dean Acheson, and many other important figures. The program was ambitious. The major goals were establishing the International Monetary Fund (IMF), opening markets around the world, and negotiating the General Agreement on Tariffs and Trade (GATT). Great Britain was fading as an economic power, and the US dollar was established as the standard currency. It was to be the first of many such conferences.

In the elegant Mount Washington dining room, Barbara DeWolfe served Lord Keynes at dinner. Mr. Adorkor, the representative from Liberia, and his wife came to dinner alone. The US senators from the South refused to allow the black couple to join their tables. Lord Keynes, seated with a Russian woman, invited the Adorkors to join them for dinner. Barbara served dinner to the two couples, an historic event for her.

Barbara was angry about racial injustice. She was strong-minded and progressive, with values similar to Mabel's. She wrote a supportive note to the Adorkors and became a small part of history. Barbara became a friend and pen pal to the Liberian couple for about twelve years. They exchanged Christmas cards; unfortunately, only one card exists. Dated December 26 (year unreadable) the colorful and beautiful card says "Silent Night" and shows the music of the carol and a church steeple. It is signed "From Mr. and Mrs. Jefferies Adorkor, Monrovia, Liberia."

The summer of 1955, when she was in her early 30s, Barbara could afford a trip to Europe, and summer jobs as a waitress ended.

Barbara had graduated from Quincy High School in 1935. There were very few professions open to women—among them was teaching. Barbara attended Bridgewater State Teachers College, and in 1939 graduated with a Bachelor of Science in Education.

In the years following Billy's death, Barbara was a constant companion to her mother. Mabel's parents had been in Los Angeles since 1919. Her father had died in 1935, leaving the elderly twins alone. In the late summer of 1941, after Eunice's elopement in March, Mabel had taken the train to

Los Angeles to look after them. For several summers Barbara traveled to Los Angeles to visit her mother and aunts. She was a welcome visitor for Mabel, a relief from the constant care of the elderly twins.

In March 1943, Amanda, "Dime," died at the age of seventy-nine. Five years later, in 1948, Amelia, "Pink," died, aged eighty-four. Mabel was the executor of their estates, which took five years to complete. B. B. Keyes had wisely invested in stocks, especially in Bullock's Department Store where he had been floor manager. He had left Mabel a generous inheritance. Again and at last, Mabel had money to spend.

Chapter 13

Return to the East
1950

In the summer of 1950, Mabel and Barbara returned to Massachusetts in a gray Plymouth Wayfarer. For almost a month beforehand, they packed hundreds of pieces of music, memorabilia, antique dishes, lamps, and paintings into boxes.

First they headed to San Francisco with two friends on July 21 for five days to celebrate Mabel's fifty-seventh birthday on July 22. On August 22, Mabel and Barbara left on their trip east.

They did sightseeing along the way and the trip took eight days. This was a fast coast-to-coast trip, considering that it was before the current network of interstates was built. Mabel recorded each day in her journal, including oil changes, gallons of gas bought, weather, and what they saw. Along the way, she notes colleges, businesses, manufacturing plants, and famous people's birthplaces.

They drove through the orange groves and crossed the Nevada state line. "Very hot," she notes. At the Arizona state line, "not good road" was her comment. They stayed overnight at the St. George Motel: "twin beds—nice—run by Mormons." They passed beautiful red sandstone formations to arrive at Zion National Park in Utah. After miles of winding road, they came to Bryce Canyon and toured its natural wonders—"breath-taking." This was followed by cattle country—"more cattle."

They toured Salt Lake City before continuing to Idaho, where they stayed in Pocatello. Continuing north and east, they crossed the Continental

Divide at Targhee Pass and descended into Montana. They entered Yellowstone at the west entrance and toured the thermal features: "Old Faithful spouted at 11:59 AM. We left after milkshake 12:25 PM."

Leaving by the south entrance, they traveled fifteen miles of narrow, often one-way road until, in the distance, they saw the Grand Tetons: "Plenty of snow in crevices." En route to Lander, Wyoming, they saw a herd of antelope; then on to Laramie and Medicine Bow and into Nebraska. Mabel notes Indian reservations and Buffalo Bill's hometown (North Platte). After Omaha, they crossed the Missouri River into Council Bluffs, Iowa: "Curvy, hilly road—lots of corn and hogs in Iowa."

It was raining in Des Moines, followed by several "bad detours" to Iowa City. Driving straight east, they entered Illinois and continued to Joliet, near Chicago. Crossing into Indiana, she noted a time change from Central to Eastern. There was a "bad truck accident" near Gary. They found a "nice motel" in Waterloo. The next day they got stuck after the rain during the night. It cost $1 to get pushed free. At the Ohio state line, they entered again Eastern Standard Time.

From Cleveland they went through Ashtabula ("Peaches") to New York state ("Lots of grapes"). They followed the south shore of Lake Erie. At Silver Creek they had logged over 10,000 miles since leaving Los Angeles. There they had to be pushed again, and the car needed new points. They went through the Finger Lakes, arrived in Albany at 2:15 in the afternoon, and immediately crossed the Hudson River into Massachusetts. Almost home!

"Beautiful drive through Berkshires." In Westfield they stopped at Howard Johnson's for "delicious fried clams." They crossed the Merrimack River at Springfield. At 8:35 p.m. on Wednesday, August 30, 1950, they rolled into north Cambridge. Home!

Barbara and Mabel rented an apartment near Grace, a sister of Billy. The following year they bought and moved into a new house on Bellevue Road in Squantum. The upstairs of the house was not yet finished when they arrived. The house was perched on a hill near the bay with a wonderful view of the water. Mabel often walked to the beach to swim.

Chapter 14
Mabel's Last Years
1951–1958

After Barbara and Mabel returned, they often took Grace DeWolfe with them on trips around New England. Grace DeWolfe Holton, Mabel's sister-in-law, was seventy-four in 1950 and still working. I remember her as haughty, unsmiling, small, and thin. She was the youngest of the DeWolfe children. When she was young, she was beautiful with blonde hair (figure 44). Born in March 1876, she married Morton Holton in 1895 at the age of nineteen. He was twenty years her senior and a typesetter for the *Boston Evening Transcript*.

Morton Holton was a Mason, very popular, and apparently happy. He loved to dance and party with friends. They had no children, and during the 1920s, the couple spent lavishly on themselves. Grace especially liked to travel. In her journal, "My Travels Abroad," she describes her "Grand Tour" on the Cunard liner the RMS *Lancastria* from June to August 19, 1929, starting and ending in New York harbor.

In 1930 Morton had a heart attack and died on the dance floor. He left Grace well off monetarily, and she continued her travels. Her money, however, did not last, and soon she began work in a yard goods store in north Cambridge, where she stayed until age seventy-eight. Ed Tappan called her a "rag peddler" and did not like her nor she him. She looked down on him. She was upper middle class and haughty. I remember visiting Great-Aunt Grace in her Cambridge apartment when I was quite young. The apartment was filled with heavy, dark Victorian furniture. A black-and-white print on the wall of a young woman looking into a mirror where she sees a skull, *Vanitas*, especially scared me. I still remember it vividly and also that Grace dwelt on the past and the fact that she was a widow alone. She ignored my presence; children were to be seen but not heard (figure 45).

After the Great Depression (1929 on), she had few financial assets. She was still working, when, aged seventy-eight, she broke her ankle in a trolley car and had to quit. This was 1958 and Mabel died that February. That summer Grace moved into Bellevue Road with Barbara. She was depressed about not being able to work. Barbara did not find her good company, as she spent most of her time in her room reading. Barbara drove off often in her car to play bridge and visit friends. Grace died in 1963 at the age of eighty-seven.

Before Grace's death, the three women traveled around New England. On a trip September 2–3, 1950, they drove into New Hampshire to North Wakefield in the Ossipees "off main road to Eunice's old house." This would have been the camp Ed inherited from Sadie and where we lived for a short time. In the winter it was very cold. I remember the outhouse and chamber pot, and a large black woodstove for heating and cooking, heavy snow in the winter and no neighbors.

Continuing to North Conway, the women found Ed at Frulize's garage where he worked. He gave them directions to the apartment he had rented. "Billy, Dickie and Barbara Louise are very cute," Mabel later wrote in her journal. This was Mabel's first sight of her grandchildren. They ate hamburgers with the family, then Ed "took us to the Drive-in Theatre." The three women stayed overnight in a motel.

In 1951 our family moved to a trailer park in Florida for a year for Ed's health. He suffered from chest and breathing problems but smoked cigars and Chesterfield cigarettes. He found work again as a mechanic in a garage. I remember the public restroom there and my fears of scorpions in it. I was six years old and attended a new elementary school with flowers in a greenhouse.

Mr. Terry, the manager of the trailer park, was a nice man who would play with me. He kept the park clean and neat. Evenings in the park, people

Chapter 14

would get together and sing popular tunes of the day to banjo and guitar. "Lady of Spain" was one. However, we children and Mother found Florida an alien place and did not like the roaches, which came out at night. The racist signs and the anger were frightening. We saw this in Georgia as well as in Florida.

Two and a half years later Mabel describes in her journal a June 25, 1952, visit with Barbara to Eunice in a trailer park in West Rye. They went to the beach where all but Mabel went swimming in the "cold water." Lunch on the beach. I remember how I hated the Rye elementary school and my unsmiling, frightening teacher.

That August, the three women made another visit to Eunice and the beach for swimming and lunch. They stopped to see Ed at the Breakfast Hill Garage where he worked. Later that month Mabel and Barbara picked up Hildegard at her home and drove to Salem, where they bought cloth at a mill and visited the House of Seven Gables and the Old Witch House. "Ate lobster in the ruff for 95 cents." Another trip that month took the same three women to the Cathedral of the Pines in New Hampshire. Mabel and Barbara took us three children to Portsmouth to shop and have ice cream before again going to the beach at Wallis Sands.

Mabel's travel journal then jumps to February 28, 1953, when, again with Hildegard, they go shopping at Shopper's World (lunch at Schrafft's), then to Marlboro, and visit a friend of Hildegard's on the way home. In April, Mabel and Barbara visited Eunice at the North Hampton Trailer Park, Whispering Pines, where we had moved. Mabel and Barbara drove to the school to pick up us children and took us for ice cream before returning to the park. The trailer had no bath tub.

The next day Mabel and Barbara picked up Thelma Sanderson, a friend, met Hildegard, who had taken the bus from Pittsfield, and drove to Sturbridge for lunch and a tour of the historic village.

Mabel and Barbara (sometimes with Grace) visited our trailer park often that summer. On August 10, they brought Billy home with them. He stayed with them until the 15th. Later that month, Grace treated Mabel, Barbara, and Thelma to dinner at the Town Line House in Peabody. On the way home they stopped at the trailer park and had to wait for Eunice to return from her job at Hytron in Massachusetts. They brought me and Barbara Louise home with them on August 25, and we stayed until September 2.

The next entry in Mabel's journal, "Places visited," is April 21, 1954, when they drove Billy to Portsmouth to have his braces tightened. Eunice did not have a driver's license. That year the trailer we rented in the park was sold, and our family moved into an old house next to the park in a section called Pine Acres. Geneva Lake Orvis was the landlady. In July we again went to Wallis Sands for a "pleasant afternoon." They brought me home with them again.

Mabel, Barbara and Hildegard traveled to Cape Cod for four days that summer, where they saw musicals, dined well, shopped, visited friends, and enjoyed many ice cream sodas at Howard Johnson's. In September they noticed much tree damage due to Hurricane Carol.

In 1955, Hildegard and Mabel visited Eunice and also took trips for pleasure. In late August, they traveled to Quebec, stopping overnight in St. Johnsbury, Vermont. In Quebec they met the cruise ship *Arosa Sun* on which Barbara and her friends, Dot and Bob, were finishing their cruise. They could not leave the boat until the next morning in order to go through Canadian customs. The five toured the city before leaving to drive home. En route they visited the Old Man and the Flume, popular attractions in Franconia Notch, New Hampshire. They walked on the boardwalk through the narrow canyon carved out by the rushing waters of the Flume. The Old Man, the profile of a face formed by rocks high above the road, has since crumbled.

In July 1956, Mabel took Eunice and family to Boston, where we rode the swan boat and went to the Museum of Science. Eunice and we boys went on the USS *Constitution*, then to the Franklin Park Zoo, and finally to meet Barbara at the Boston University School of Education library. In August Mabel, Barbara, Barbara Louise, and I drove to New Salem to visit a family. In the fall, Barbara took us bowling at Hampton Beach. "A very lovely drive and a perfect fall day."

Chapter 14

The year 1957 brought summer visits to North Hampton and various tours around Massachusetts. The last entry in Mabel's journal is dated Sunday, November 10, 1957—Barbara Louise's birthday party. Mabel and Barbara arrived late morning at Eunice's, bringing a cake and a red-and-white dress, red sweater, pixie hat, and mittens for the birthday girl. At the party also were an Italian family and two children from the trailer park. After watching *Wide, Wide World*, they left for home around 5:30 p.m.

While she traveled around New England and visited her daughter and family, Mabel continued her musical career. The Beralde Trio, founded in 1933, came together again and played many gigs. The same three women made up the trio: Mabel on violin, Hildegard Berthold on cello, and Agnes Ruggles Allen on piano. They played again in churches, especially for Easter and Christmas, for dramatic performances, in private homes, in schools—many places. For eight years, Mabel, Hildegard, and Agnes were happy again.

In the center of Quincy is Bethany Congregational Church, with one thousand parishioners. Located on the corner of Coddington and Spear streets, the church is a grand Gothic building with a high tower and distinctive gargoyles. Mabel especially liked the stained glass windows. The Bethany Players were the centerpiece of the church's music programs. At the holidays, they would put on ambitious performances with actors, singers, and musicians. The Beralde Trio was often part of these performances.

An April 1, 1956, Easter program was typical of the performances at the church. The *Quincy Patriot Ledger* reported that, "the Beralde String Trio will be accompanied by organ preludes at both services and will accompany the choirs during their anthems." *Alleluia* was another ambitious performance, with about forty singers, actresses and actors taking part. The program proudly announced that, "This Drama is produced by special arrangement with the Walter M. Baker Company, Boston, Massachusetts."

The trio played in other area churches such as the Wollaston Congregational Church and the Parkway Community Church. They played for vespers and weddings as well as for holiday performances. In addition to churches, the trio was popular for graduations, such as those of the Boston School of Nursing.

Even in her 60s Mabel continued to be a fine, professional performer. She was punctual and organized. Many detailed lists of pieces played, when and where and by whom remain today. Mabel loved her work even when arthritic fingers caused her pain.

She was unusual as a woman violinist in a field still dominated by men. At that time, 98% of professional violinists were male. In her last years, Mabel was a loving and supportive grandmother as well as a musician. She didn't like it when her grandchildren were taken to Florida for a year. However, in her journals she did not express her feelings. She remained a private person.

On February 6, 1958, Mabel DeWolfe drove into Quincy to her dentist. Both she and Billy had many dental problems during their lifetimes, probably because of the high sugar in their diets. Mabel loved her cake and ice cream. She had had many teeth pulled and replaced with bridges. This time she was suffering from gingivitis, and the dentist was ready to pull more teeth. Maybe it was the bad news from the dentist, but on the way home, at a stop sign, she suddenly opened the car door and then slumped over the steering wheel, blowing the horn several times. She was sixty-five years old when she died.

Her violin would remain silent for seventeen years. Barbara kept the violin made by Jacob Thoma in Boston in 1904, and only in 1975 gave it to Eunice, who was, like her mother, an excellent violinist. Today, the violin is played by our daughter, Mandy, Mabel's great-grand-daughter (figure 46).

Chapter 15

After Mabel
1958–2016

The summer after Mabel's death, Grace moved into Bellevue Road with Barbara because of her broken ankle. They lived together until 1963, when Grace died at the age of eighty-seven. In the summer of 2001, Barbara sold the house and moved to Langdon Place, a retirement home in Exeter, New Hampshire. In 2013, Barbara died shortly before her ninety-fifth birthday. She is buried in Quincy, next to her parents, Billy and Mabel DeWolfe.

Barbara never married, but Eunice and Ed Tappan had three children: Billy, born January 31, 1942; Richard (myself), born July 20, 1945; and Barbara Louise, born November 10, 1946.

In 1941, Edwin Elden Tappan was drafted into the US Navy for a year. Eunice was pregnant and without her husband. While serving at sea, he became very sick with pneumonia combined with influenza, and eventually was honorably discharged. Over thirty years later, Ed developed cancer in his right eye. I remember seeing him welding and a spark striking that eye. The tumor spread into the brain, and for eight long years Eunice cared for him in their home in North Hampton. Eventually, the doctors operated and cut out his right eye, leaving him disfigured and legally blind due to cataracts in his left eye. The cancer spread to other parts of his body, and Ed died on July 13, 1973, age sixty-five.

Ed's long illness took a toll on Eunice's health. About three years later, in 1975, Eunice became transformed and happy, when she married Albert Copp, a friend and neighbor, whose wife had died. Albert Copp was good at skiing, and he had won the Purple Heart in World War II. When Al was young, he had joined the 10th Mountain Division in Italy.

The couple moved to Exeter, where they lived for twenty-five years. Eunice and Al supported each other, and their marriage flourished. Almost every Sunday, Al and Eunice went to the Baptist church in Exeter. Eunice took up the violin again (when Barbara gave her Mabel's violin) and began doing watercolors.

Eunice painted many scenes of the New England coast, such as the Nubble Lighthouse in southern Maine and surrounding rocks and beaches. At the York (Maine) Art Association, Eunice exhibited many of her watercolors and felt gratified about her accomplishments. She exhibited also in the Exeter Hospital and many other settings. Al encouraged Eunice in her painting and music. She began playing violin with Amanda, her granddaughter.

In 2001, Eunice fell downstairs while Barbara DeWolfe was visiting, and everything changed for the worse. Eunice was taken to the hospital unconscious, and Al had a major heart attack at the hospital. Thankfully, Al survived.

For three years, Eunice was on dialysis and slowly declining. She died in an Exeter nursing home in the fall of 2004, at the age of eighty-four. In the living room of their house, an unfinished painting by Eunice remained on an easel. Al eventually died of pneumonia at the age of eighty-four in 2008. They are buried together in Exeter.

Today, Eunice and Ed's children are grown, married, and with children of their own. Bill lives in Eliot, Maine, with his third wife, Nancy. (Bill's first wife, Judy, died in childbirth at age nineteen; Bill was twenty. He later married and then divorced Esther.) His children are Bill, Jr.; Robert; Elizabeth; Douglas; and Mark.

Barbara Louise married Howard Colvin, who had a daughter, Wendy, by a previous marriage. He died in 1998. They had no children and Barbara did not remarry.

I live in Dover with my wife Sally. Our children are Melissa (Missy), born March 7, 1972; Amanda (Mandy), born March 11, 1974; and Richard, Jr.,

Chapter 15

born March 15, 1977. Melissa and her husband, Andy Parr, live in Newburyport with children Alex, Abigail, Max, Jack and Sammy. Mandy and her husband, Sam Tombarelli, live in Portsmouth with two daughters, Sophie and Evangelina (Evie.) Richard (Rick) and his wife Elizabeth live in Helena, Montana, with children Jeremiah, Elise, Forrest, and Sylvia Rose—with a fifth expected soon. Rick graduated *cum laude* from Gonzaga University Law School and was hired by a law firm in Helena. Together, Sally and I will have twelve grandchildren.

Music continues in the family. In 2005, the all-woman chamber trio, Trillium, was formed, made up of violin, piano or organ, and flute. Like the Beralde Trio, they perform at churches, weddings, and similar settings. Mandy plays Mabel's violin, Melanie Sobotka plays the flute, Jan Stover plays the piano and organ. Trillium performs classical, Celtic, and contemporary music in southern Maine, New Hampshire, and Massachusetts. Mandy's daughters are learning the violin by the Suzuki method. Sam, on the other hand, carries on the painting tradition by working in oils. Max, Missy's son, is also learning to play the violin and is a purple belt in karate. Alex plays the guitar, and Abby plays the piano.

The musical and theatrical tradition of Billy and Mabel DeWolfe is carried on today by their children and grandchildren. Billy and Mabel would be proud. The boxes of letters, journals, photographs, paintings, posters, and other memorabilia, preserved by the family members, made possible this family history. These documents and artifacts form a museum of memories.

Illustrations

FIGURE 1. B. B. Keyes' pass for admission to the Columbian Exposition in Chicago, October 31, 1893

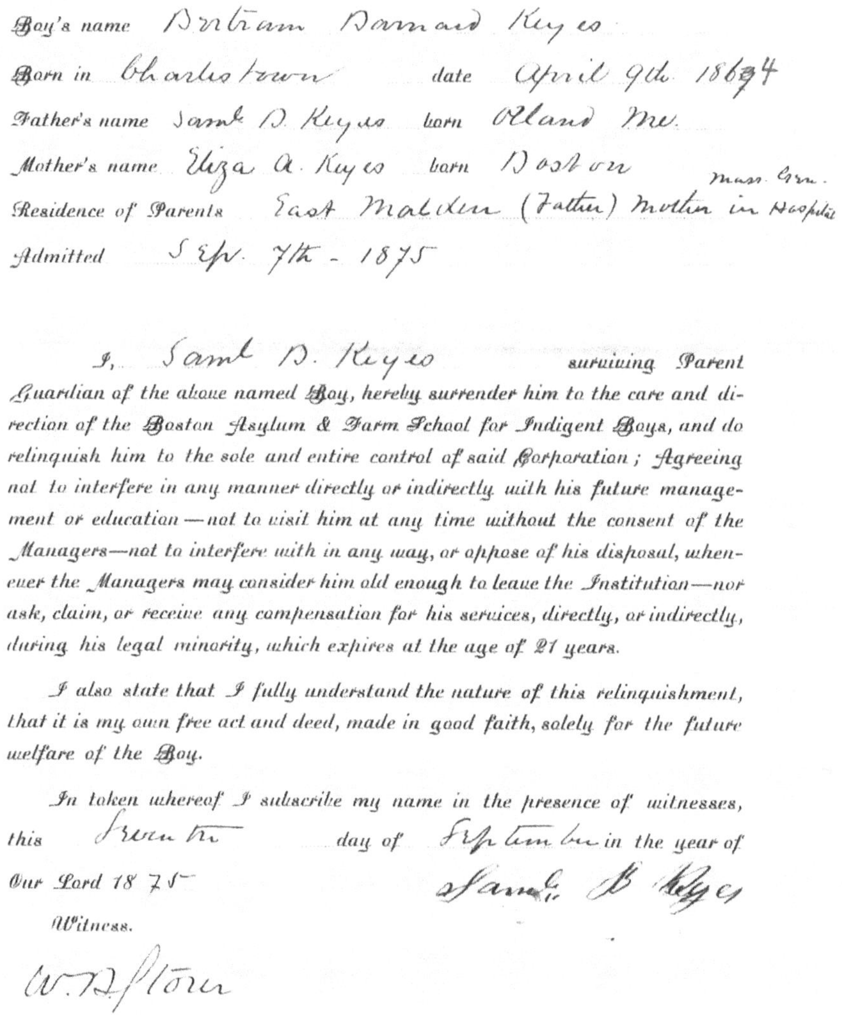

Boy's name Bertram Barnard Keyes
Born in Charlestown   date April 9th 1869 [4]
Father's name Sam'l B. Keyes born Orland Me.
Mother's name Eliza A. Keyes born Boston   Mass. Gen.
Residence of Parents East Malden (Father) Mother in Hospital
Admitted Sep. 7th - 1875

I, Sam'l B. Keyes surviving Parent Guardian of the above named Boy, hereby surrender him to the care and direction of the Boston Asylum & Farm School for Indigent Boys, and do relinquish him to the sole and entire control of said Corporation; Agreeing not to interfere in any manner directly or indirectly with his future management or education — not to visit him at any time without the consent of the Managers — not to interfere with in any way, or oppose of his disposal, whenever the Managers may consider him old enough to leave the Institution — nor ask, claim, or receive any compensation for his services, directly, or indirectly, during his legal minority, which expires at the age of 21 years.

I also state that I fully understand the nature of this relinquishment, that it is my own free act and deed, made in good faith, solely for the future welfare of the Boy.

In token whereof I subscribe my name in the presence of witnesses, this Seventh day of September in the year of Our Lord 18 75

Sam'l B. Keyes

Witness.
W. D. Storer

FIGURE 2. Document of relinquishment of his son to the Boston Farm and Trade School, signed by Samuel Keyes, dated September 7, 1875

FIGURE 3. First page of Supplement to the Thompson's Island School newspaper, the *Beacon*, describing the history of its printing press, July 1911

CORNET SOLOIST OF THE FAMOUS
SALEM CADET BAND.

CORNET VIRTUOSO.

Bertrand B. Keyes

CAN BE ENGAGED AS

Soloist for Concerts, Church and all First
Class Entertainments.

Teacher of the Cornet and Military Bands.
Arranger of Music for Military Bands and Orchestras.

Salem, Mass., Feb. 17th 1898

Mr. C. H. Bradley.
  Boston Mass.
Dear Sir—

Your letter of the 9th also the literature & received with much pleasure. Although being away from the school, now quite a few years and in that time having traveled across the country from one ocean to the other also north and south I still cherish the same kind remembrance of the old school as though it was but yesterday that I left its protecting arms. It has not been my pleasure now for a good many years to visit the school one reason was that I have not been in this part of the country.

FIGURE 4. First page of a letter from B. B. Keyes to Charles H. Bradley, Superintendent of the Thompson's Island Farm School, February 19, 1898

Figure 5. Photo taken in 1886 when the Philbrick twins were twenty-two years old. In center seated is Amelia ("Pink"), standing is Amanda ("Dime"). On either side are sisters Georgia and Sue.

Figure 6. Amelia, B. B., and baby Mabel Keyes, 1894

FIGURE 7. The electric tower at the Pan-American Exposition, 1901, by day and by night (Barry, Richard H., *The Grandeurs of the Exposition*, Buffalo, NY: R. A. Reid, 1901, n.p.)

FIGURE 8A. Postcard to Mabel Keyes from a family friend, 1903

FIGURE 8B. Postcard to Mabel from Beatrice, a fellow musician 1907

FIGURE 8C. Another postcard from Beatrice to Mabel Keyes, 1907

FIGURE 8D. Postcard to Mabel from a friend, 1907

(See back cover for color images.)

Figure 9. Mabel Keyes at twenty-two on the cover of the December 1915 Longergan Players program

Figure 10. Mabel Keyes (second from left, seated) in an all-women musical ensemble, May 7, 1913. Mabel was twenty years old.

FIGURE 11. Postcard from Billy from Plymouth, Massachusetts, to Mabel in Lynn, June 1917: "Miss my Babe… Lots of Love."

Figure 12. Billy's parents Isiah DeWolfe and Ellen Barbara (MacDonald), 1880s

Figure 13. Billy DeWolfe's sisters: (left to right) Laura, Grace, Elizabeth, Jenny and Eunice (seated) (n.d.)

Figure 14. Billy DeWolfe in costume. Photo taken circa 1900, when Billy was about twenty-six.

Figure 15. Mabel and baby Ellen Barbara, 1919

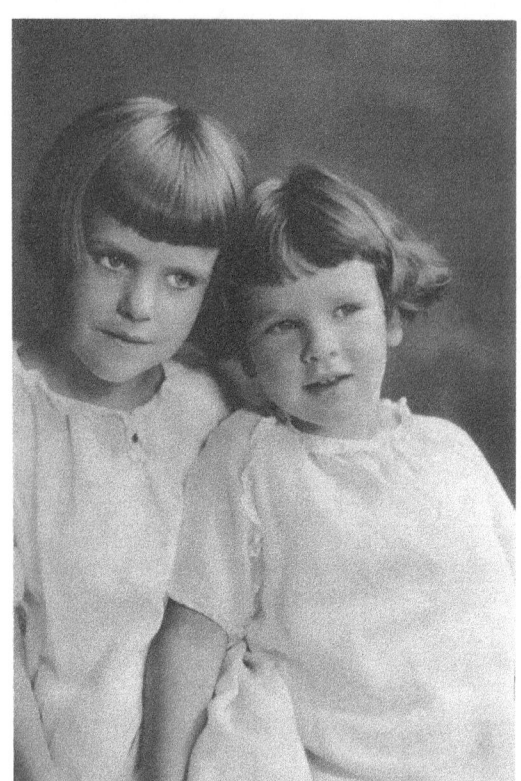

Figure 16. Barbara (left) and Eunice DeWolfe, December 25, 1924. Barbara was six and Eunice was four.

Figure 17. Young Barbara DeWolfe, circa 1924, demonstrating a new invention, the public pay phone, in Quincy.

DeWOLFE BACK IN KNICKERS!

"Billy" Opines That Folks at Boothbay Harbor Will Welcome Him, Despite 'Em

QUINCY, Aug 8—"Billy" DeWolfe, manager of a local theatre, has gone to his native town, Boothbay Harbor, Me, "knickers" and all. Probably nobody who ever left Boothbay Harbor—and, mind you, there is all the difference in the world between Boothbay and Boothbay Harbor, and make no mistake—says Billy, who ever gets such a real reception back home when he "gits" there. Billy, as a boy, was forever getting up theatrical shows in his father's barn when the father was off to sea, for which he charged pins, nails and other commodities in the hardware and nursery line.

The DeWolfes for generations before him had the call of the sea in their blood, but Billy had the call of the stage, and stagewards he went. The thousands of people who have seen "Way Down East" will remember the fat chore boy who used to read jokes out of a patent medicine almanac and eat a big red apple in every performance. Away back before the days of the celluloid drama, Billy was the "High Roller" of the show and the envy of every boy and girl who saw it because he had bright, shiny new apples given him to eat at every performance.

Well, Billy has gone along the road some since that time. Within the past week he even dared to wear "knickers" in this town where everybody thinks well of him. He declared he would wear them to Boothbay Harbor or bust; perhaps he may do both. The last time he was in Boothbay Harbor he had his picture snapped standing against the house in which he was born. "Quincy may have the birthplaces of two Presidents," said Billy, "but when I get back to that city I'll show them that Boothbay Harbor also produced a great man, and also the house in which he was born."

Neither Billy nor the amateur photographer who was taking the picture realized that the roll of films had run out when the button was pressed, but both knew it when the film was developed. It produced a blank space.

And Billy was just good enough sport to tell the story on himself because that's the kind of a fellow he is and that is why hundreds of Quincy people are hoping he will enjoy his vacation.

FIGURE 18. Article in the *Quincy Patriot Ledger* describing Billy's visit to his hometown, Boothbay, Maine (n.d.)

FIGURE 19. An advertisement for Mabel's band, the Wolverines. Mabel is in the center with her violin. A handwritten note by her refers to the Beralde Trio: "Can also furnish a first class trio for all occasions."

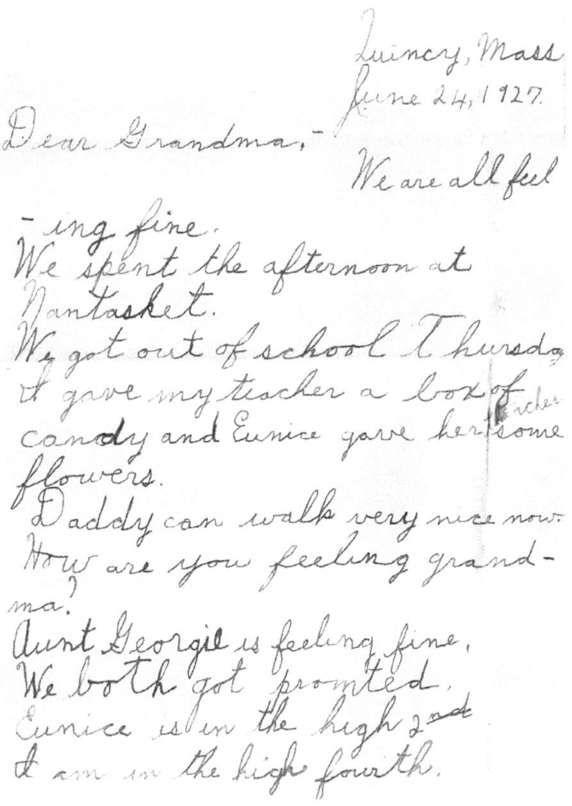

Figure 20. Letter from Barbara, eight and a half years old, to Amelia, June 24, 1927

> Quincy, Mass
> June 24, 1927.
>
> Dear Grandma,-
> We are all feeling fine.
> We spent the afternoon at Nantasket.
> We got out of school Thursday. I gave my teacher a box of richer candy and Eunice gave her some flowers.
> Daddy can walk very nice now.
> How are you feeling grandma?
> Aunt Georgie is feeling fine.
> We both got promoted. Eunice is in the high 2nd I am in the high fourth.
> My teacher's name is Miss Frances Sullivan. 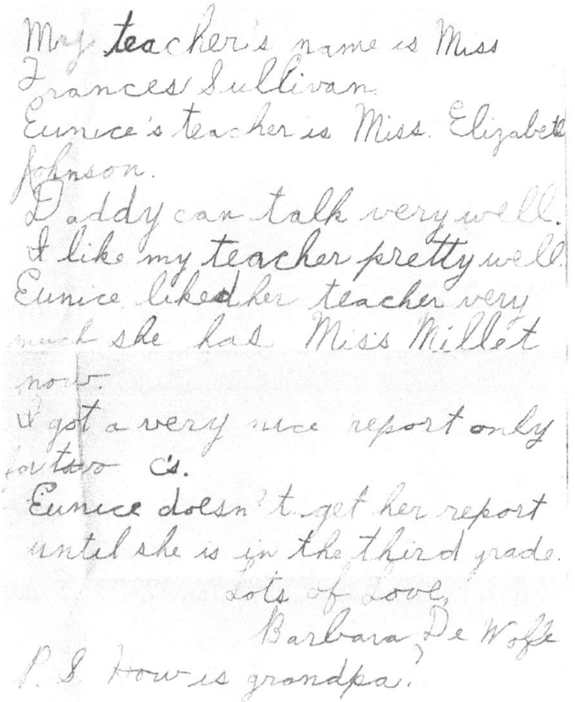
> Eunice's teacher is Miss Elizabeth Johnson.
> Daddy can talk very well.
> I like my teacher pretty well.
> Eunice liked her teacher very much she has Miss Millet now.
> I got a very nice report only for two C's.
> Eunice doesn't get her report until she is in the third grade.
>   Lots of Love,
>   Barbara De Wolfe
> P.S. How is grandpa?

JOHN G. MUNRO
BEDFORD BUILDING
MIAMI, FLORIDA

Sunday Night, February 20, 1927.

Will - Billy - Biff - dear good friend of my youth - is it of thee, oh, strong man, Hercules, of the old crowd - Jimmy, Will, Frank Tighe, Harry Moore and John G. - is it of thee I read that thy great strength, and will and courage unsurpassed, has like the rest of us to acknowledge the untiring efforts, the earnest and ceaseless work you always put in to your day has at last notified you you must exercise rest, and treat yourself as a human being.

Few are they who have worked harder, honester, sincerer, Will. Your record is clear as crystal. In a busy, hustling life you have gathered only friends.

The item in last night's Traveler proves that. No man I can this moment name could call to his banner a list of finer people - of greater talent. All honor to them, Will, and you are worthy of it.

I have written all day to as many of the Old Guard as I can recall or reach and we'll be there tomorrow night, Will, just as you have been a dozen of dozen times for others.

Be of good cheer, Will. There's a lot of fight in you yet. Your courage will carry on till the old strength returns to restore you to the enjoyment of the activities you enjoyed so well.

Lill and myself extend to you, dear Will, and to Mrs. DeWolfe, our earnest and prayerfull wishes for a speedy and complete return to you of your usual good health.

You are all right, Will, and you'll win out this time as you have before. Do not permit yourself to worry because you don't need to. The enclosed may help along that last line.

Three rousing cheers, Will, we are all with you,

John G.

PRIVATE OFFICE
QUINCY HOUSE
BOSTON, MASS.

Mr. William W. De Wolfe,
30 Chicatawbut Road,
Quincy, Mass.

TO INSURE PROMPT DELIVERY PLEASE ADDRESS ANSWER TO P. O. BOX 793, MIAMI, FLORIDA

FIGURE 21. Letter of condolence and encouragement to Billy after his stroke from John Munro, an old friend, February 20, 1927

"BILL" DeWOLFE IS GIVEN BIG SURPRISE BY MANY FRIENDS

A Christmas tree which was adorned with approximately 200 cards expressing original sentiments and signed by those who extended them, graced the living room of the home of William W. DeWolfe on Christmas day and gave added cheer to that well known theatrical man who is gradually recovering from an illness which has required treatment the past three months.

Each card was separately attached to the tree by red or green ribbon, or silvered string. Surmounted by a Chistmas star the tree made a most effective appearance.

It was presented to "Bill" when he joined the family at Christmas dinner. Later in the afternoon it was his privilege to have the cards read to him. They gave him laugh after laugh.

The cards were inscribed by many of his best friends, including people prominent in the business district where "Bill" has been as much a factor as any other man actively connected with it.

FIGURE 22. A Christmas surprise, 1927, *Quincy Patriot Ledger*

ACTOR LAUDS DE WOLFE AT OPPORTUNITY NIGHT SHOW

Says He Is Best Manager On Earth. Well Pleased With Fine Program Put On At Quincy Theatre Last Night. Local Acts Well Received.

"The Quincy Theatre has the best manager in God's Green earth" was the tribute paid to "Billy" DeWolfe last night by "Bob" Alexander, a member of one of the acts, from the stage of the Quincy Theatre.

HUNDREDS AT TESTIMONIAL TO DE WOLFE

Miss Georgette Cohan and "Bossy" Gillis Head Big Midnight Show Bill

CUNNINGHAM TOPS BILL AT BIG DEWOLFE NIGHT

FRED ALLEN TO HEAD BILL AT DEWOLFE TESTIMONIAL

Star of 'Little Show' to Appear at Midnight Show at Strand Theatre—Jimmie Gallagher Included on Big 12-act Bill

Greenwich Village Follies Star In DeWolfe Testimonial Show

Dr.' Rockwell, Heads Bill For Midnight Performance At Quincy Theater Thursday Night— Other Stars Promised

FIGURE 23. Headlines of articles in the *Quincy Patriot Ledger* about the annual testimonial dinners and performances for Billy DeWolfe, held 1928–1931

FIGURE 24. Publicity photo of Mabel, probably taken in the early 1930s.

DECEMBER 11, 1930

MABEL K. DEWOLFE LEADS ORCHESTRA

Quincy boasts of a woman who is not only a musician of repute, but who leads an orchestra, a band and a string ensemble, comprised entirely of women musicians. To hundreds of Quincy and South Shore patrons of the Quincy Theatre, she is known as Mabel K. DeWolfe but in private life she is the wife of William K. DeWolfe of Quincy, well-known theatrical manager.

Mrs. DeWolfe is a violinist, and previous to coming to the Quincy Theatre seven years ago, led other theatre orchestras. At the present time she is devoting much of her time to teaching and ensemble work. The "Wolverines," a string ensemble of which she is conductor, has filled many engagements of importance. Recently Mrs. DeWolfe used a special arrangement of the violin, 'cello, organ and harp for the special Christmas service at the Needham Congregational church.

FIGURE 25. A *Quincy Patriot Ledger* article of December, 1930, praises Mabel as a professional female musician and wife of Billy DeWolfe.

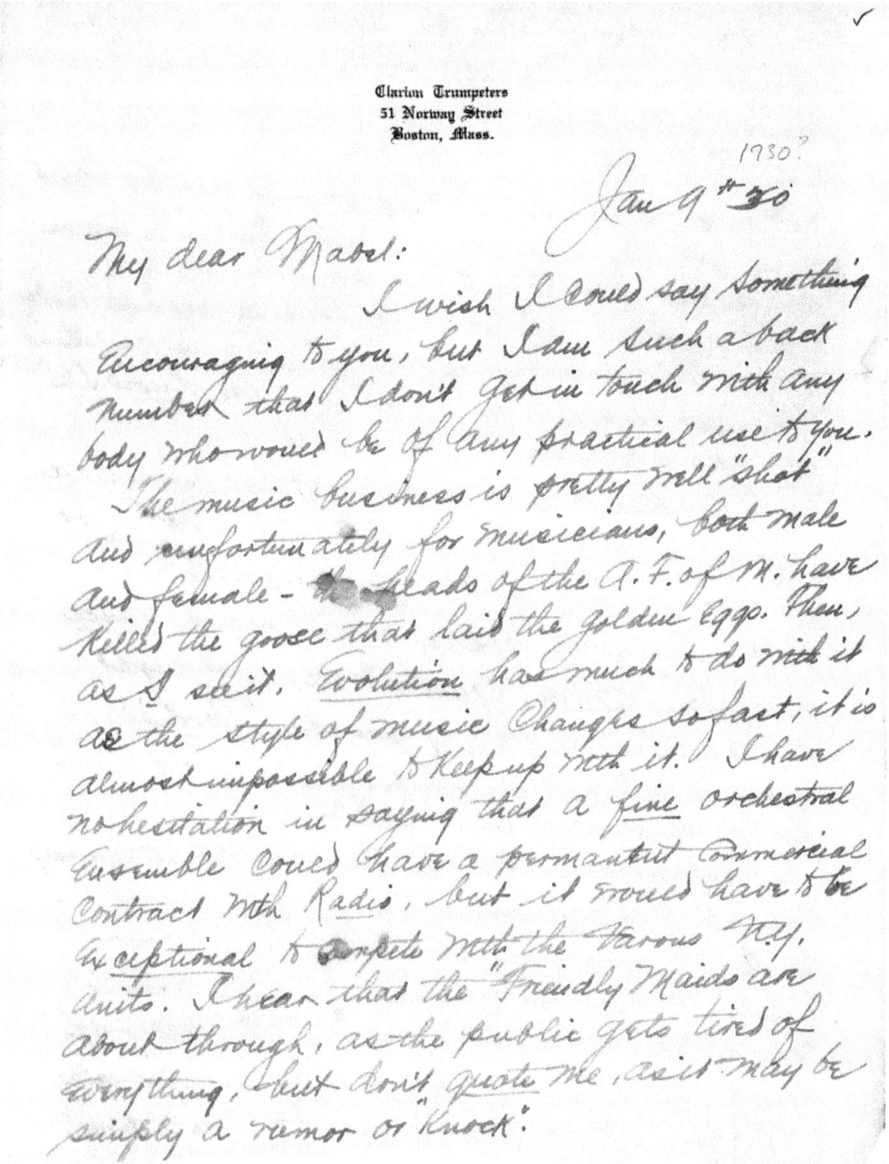

Clarion Trumpeters
51 Norway Street
Boston, Mass.

1930?

Jan 9th 30

My dear Mabel:

I wish I could say something encouraging to you, but I am such a back number that I don't get in touch with anybody who would be of any practical use to you. The music business is pretty well "shot" and unfortunately for musicians, both male and female — the heads of the A. F. of M. have killed the goose that laid the golden eggs. Then, as I said, Evolution has much to do with it as the style of music changes so fast, it is almost impossible to keep up with it. I have no hesitation in saying that a *fine* orchestral Ensemble could have a permanent Commercial Contract with Radio, but it would have to be exceptional to compete with the various N.Y. units. I hear that the "Friendly Maids" are about through, as the public gets tired of everything, but don't quote me, as it may be simply a rumor or "knock".

Figure 26. First page of letter to Mabel from fellow musician, Caroline Nichols, January 9, 1930

Clarion Trumpeters
51 Norway Street
Boston, Mass.

January 9, [19]30

My dear Mabel,

I wish I could say something encouraging to you, but I am such a back number that I don't get in touch with anybody who would be of any practical use to you.

The music business is pretty well "shot" and unfortunately for musicians, both male and female, the heads of the A.F. of M. [American Federation of Musicians] have killed the goose that laid the golden eggs. Then, as I see it, Evolution has much to do with it as the style of music changes so fast, it is almost impossible to keep up with it. I have no hesitation in saying that a fine orchestral ensemble could have a permanent commercial contract with Radio, but it would have to be exceptional to compete with the various N.Y. units. I hear that the "Friendly Maids" are about through, as the public gets tired of everything, but don't quote me, as it may be simply a rumor or "knock."

The "Talkies" seem to be in the ascendant just now and I doubt if Vaudeville ever comes back, but one never knows! You know every dog has his day, and only Time stays,--we go!

I really think that teaching is your best bet, as it seems to be the only reliable job a woman musician can expect to hold and you are your own boss.

It's a rotten shame that such a capable leader as you are has to loaf, and if there is anything I can do at any time to help you, you know I'll be happy to do it.

I enclose a little magazine that comes to me regularly, and it would do no harm to insert an "add" for club work, teas, receptions, etc. Emphasize your ability to do concert, dance, & theatrical work equally well. It might

FIGURE 27. Transcript of letter from Caroline Nichols

possibly help a little if you say, "Cordially endorsed by C.B.N. as exceptionally well fitted for all musical requirements"—

Also, I would see the Rec. Sec. of the Quincy Woman's Club & borrow her official list of the N.E. Women's Clubs--& send one of your circulars to each one of them – I presume their calendar for the season is filled, but most of them close the season with a "blow-out" (generally a flat tire [?], too) Gentlemen's Night and hire a prof. orchestra for concert and dance – I used to do lots of these affairs, but I could not get a team like yours that I could depend on to do the work right & behave themselves, so I gave it up –

It wouldn't take much gas to run from Quincy to Hingham and shall expect you next summer. Very glad "Billy" is improving—tell him I know how hard it is to be patient under such conditions, and courage oozes out of my finger tips that are getting stiff & numb.

Life now-a-days is just one damn thing after another—the repair men, fixing the roof, knocked down my antenna, short circuited my radio & burned it all out—useless, and doubt if it can be repaired, it was such a fine set and my only joy in life!

I'm afraid I haven't said much to help you, but you can "take it for what it's worth" as the man said when the jackass kicked him!

Best regards & hopes for a better New Year than the last.

Cordially yours,

Caroline B. Nichols alias "Teacher"

FAREWELL TO QUINCY

"Strange Interlude" will leave Quincy tonight after a run of four weeks, during which the Theatre Guild turned 'em away, and will pursue its sinister course to Springfield. After shocking that fair cathedral town, the insatiable Nina will appall Rochester and Cleveland and then defile Chicago for as long a period as the city can stand the defilement. Quincy seems to have withstood the shock very well. The sheeted dead have not burst the granite barriers of their tombs in the presidential church. Mayor McGrath and the restaurateurs are sitting pretty, and a good time was had by all.

Persons with a sordid financial soul may now reflect on the box office aspects of the play if it had come to Boston. Quincy was good for four weeks. How long would the play have lasted in Boston? At least eight weeks, probably twelve, and possibly the whole season. Few persons living north of Boston went to Quincy by motor or rail. Many Bostonians who would have gone to the Hollis Street theatre did not take the trouble of going to the South Shore.

"Strange Interlude" offers a variety of thrills which are unrelated to the merits of the play itself. The novelty of going to the theatre in the afternoon, coming out to dine and returning for the rest of the evening would have drawn throngs. Intellectual and social Boston has lost considerable, and the specialty shops, department stores, haberdashers, florists, taxis, garages, etc., are out thousands of dollars.

FIGURE 28. A witty commentary published in the *Quincy Patriot Ledger* after the successful run of "Strange Interlude," 1929

'Billy' DeWolfe Expires After Long Sickness

DEATH RINGS DOWN CURTAIN FOR DEWOLFE

Merrymount Man Nationally Known as Outstanding Stage Comedian

FIGURE 29. Headlines announcing Billy's death in September, 1932

FIGURE 30. Autographed photo of James Cagney: "To Mabel K. DeWolfe, Sincerely, James Cagney"

Figure 31. A signed publicity photo of Billy De Wolfe, Jr., dated 1925 on back.

Figure 32. Billy De Wolfe, Jr., as part of the DeWolfe family. Billy, Eunice and Barbara in front of the home in Merrymount, 1937.

Figure 33. Billy and Barbara teasing each other, 1950

Figure 34. Autographed photo: "To my 'Sis,' Barbara— Wishing you only the best! Billy De Wolfe" (n. d.)

FIGURE 35. From Mabel's scrapbook: Billy De Wolfe, Jr., sails for Europe, 1932.

MRS. MURGATROYD SAILS: Comedian Billy De-Wolfe, formerly of Wollaston, poses aboard the Queen Elizabeth, before sailing for Europe. He will give a four week performance at the Cafe de Paris, go to Glasgow, Edinburgh and return to London to appear at the Palladium late in July.   (Cunard Line photograph) 1932

FIGURE 36. From Mabel's scrapbook: Billy with co-stars Dorothy Lamour and Bing Crosby, 1943.

BILLY DeWOLFE OF QUINCY, center, who is coming to the Strand theatre in "Dixie" on Aug. 18, 19, 20 and 21, is shown above in a scene from the current technicolor musical film hit with co-stars Dorothy Lamour and Bing Crosby. The Quincy stage and screen star plays the part of Mr. Bones in "Dixie" and really steals the picture from such veteran performers as the beauteous Lamour and the one and only Bing.

PARAMOUNT PICTURES INC.
WEST COAST STUDIOS
5451 MARATHON ST. HOLLYWOOD, CALIF.
TELEPHONE HOLLYWOOD 2411 CABLE ADDRESS PAMFILM

555 No. Rossmore
Hollywood 4,
Oct. 15, 1946

Dear Mrs De Wolfe:-
Please excuse me for not writing sooner but it seems I go from one picture to another—
Just finished "Dear Ruth" with Joan Caulfield and go into "Variety Girl" next—
And of late I have been doing radio shows Was on the Ginny Simms show last Friday Oct. 11 and next Monday Oct 21 am on the Lux Radio show doing "Susie Slagle".
Did you see Life Mag. last week, a wonderful break for me! Blue Skies is the Xmas attraction.
I missed getting home this summer but hope to make it next May—
Hope you are well, and give my best Barbara—
All good wishes,
Billy

FIGURE 37. Letter to Mabel from Billy De Wolfe, Jr., October 15, 1946

Quincy Still First With Billy DeWolfe

Film Actor Spends Holiday Here With Aunt

BY MABELLE FULLERTON

Billy de Wolfe, Quincy's star-spangled gift to the entertainment world, whom his friend Bing Crosby describes as "the hottest thing in pictures," left for Hollywood today after spending Christmas in Quincy with his aunt, Miss Laura Jones of 22 South Central avenue, Wollaston. With three films lined up for him as soon as he returns to Hollywood Billy doesn't expect to be back "home" for a year and a half.

In Crosby Picture

With Bing Crosby he has just completed work on the $3,000,000 Paramount production of "Blue Skies" in which Irving Berlin's music forms the background. Berlin wrote a special song for Billy's use but he explains "I didn't think it was especially funny and the spot was such a good one I suggested 'Mrs. Murgatroyd' which I developed during my night club engagements. Gary Cooper dropped in during the scene and laughed so much, we had to do a retake. When . . ." (DeWolfe)

Turn to Page Seven

THE LAUGH that stopped a $3,000,000 production: Gary Cooper, right, arrives on the "Blue Skies" Paramount lot to visit Bing Crosby, left, and to hear Billy de Wolfe, Quincy film comedian do "Mrs. Murgatroyd." Stuart Heisler, director is the center figure.

FIGURE 38. Article in the *Quincy Patriot Ledger* about the stars of *Blue Skies*, 1946

Billy DeWolfe Works Quincy Into His New Musical Revue

By Mary R. Coolidge

"How is everything in Quincy?" was the first question asked by Wollaston's Billy DeWolfe, famous nightclub, motion picture, stage and TV star, yesterday when interviewed, just a few short hours from opening curtain-time of John Murray Anderson's musical revue "Almanac" which had its premiere last night at the Shubert Theater in Boston.

Plug For Quincy

"I never forget Quincy," he continued, "as a matter of fact I had lunch Wednesday with Governor Herter and I certainly put in a plug for Quincy, and Quincy has three places in the show. In one particular sketch 'Little Women' the name Quincy has been substituted for Tulsa in the song as originally scored, and in two other sketches I manage to bring in the name again . . ."

He was very proud to admit that he is 20 pounds lighter and six inches trimmer around the waist, which is the result of a diet the past few weeks, as he said, "You can't wear an 18th Century form-fitting costume with a bay-window in the front."

Another thing, he has shaved off his famous mustache, which has been one of his famous characteristics, and he intends to keep it off, as he seems to like it better and so do his friends.

One of the most repeated queries to Billy is, "Are you going to do Mrs. Mrygatroyd?"— which is, of course, practically one of his trademarks—"No, I am not doing that sketch in this show," he said gaily. "She is on vacation getting a well earned rest."

"I have been rehearsing like mad since arriving in Boston, but I love every minute of it," he said "This show is a musical revue, different from a musical comedy, which h a book or plot, but, it is typical of any John Murray Anderson's productions— it is absolutely fabulous! Just judging from the magnificent costumes and the scenery, not to say a thing about the revues, it is shaping up like the 'best of the best' Ziegfeld Follies More than 150 members are in the cast, each working like crazy to give their best in the show, and all the girls are both beautiful and talented. Miss Hermonie Gingold, English comedienne, who is co-starring with me, is one of the funniest I have worked with, and on and on all through the large cast.

"After opening the show in a regular business suit, I have about five minutes to dash back to my dressing room, (which, incidentally, and rightfully, is room No. 1 with a large silver star) where my valet, William Cooke, is waiting, acting as my dresser, whip-change into my costume and on again . . . and this goes on all throughout the show."

Gesturing around the room, you well agree that this must be one of the most exciting parts of backstage exciting drama, as the walls and racks are literally lined high with costume changes, dungarees, army fatigues, century costumes, gas mask, dozens of wigs, mountain-climbing garments, top hats, dress suit and many, many more, all complete with accessories from boots to sneakers.

In one sketch with Miss Gingold he wears a hysterically funny female garb of pale pink silk, lace fischu at the neckline, strings of pearls and a daring top-piece of flowers and gadgets, which is the identical costume worn recently by Ed Wynn on his TV show with Miss Gingold.

He shook his head a little sadly when mention was made of some Quincy theaters and he voiced his regrets that TV is making the people stay at home to watch some of the most famous stars, in every theatrical field, of this age. But he brightened up again and flashed his famous smile when the Wollaston School was brought into the subject (as that was where he went to school) and other places of interest of which he has so many pleasant memories.

Scores of telegrams and messages of good luck were being brought into his dressing room, for the few moments he relaxed yesterday between sketch rehearsals, but all together none can compare to the sincerity of the "well wishes" from his good neighbors in Quincy.

WHAT'S MISSING?—Billy DeWolfe's famous mustache, which he has shaved off, as shown while he was being assisted in trying on one of his costumes by his valet William Cook, in his dressing room at the Shubert Theater in Boston. DeWolfe is starring in John Murray Anderson's "Almanac" musical revue, which opened last night. (Charles Flagg Photo)

FIGURE 39. Article in the *Quincy Patriot Ledger* about Billy DeWolfe, Jr., and his hometown, Quincy, November 6, 1953

FIGURE 40. Mabel on left and Barbara on right with Billy in front of his dressing room at Paramount Pictures, 1946

FIGURE 41. Paramount Pictures publicity photo of a scene from *Miss Susie Slagle* with Billy De Wolfe, Jr., and Lillian Gish (n.d.)

GOODBYE, BILLY -- Miss Bessie Powers [left], his childhood teacher at the Wollaston School, dabs at tears, as interment services for comedian-actor Billy DeWolfe are completed at Mount Wollaston Cemetery Monday.

[Quincy Sun Photo by Laban H. Whittaker]

Simple Services Here

Billy DeWolfe: 'He Brought So Much Into Lives Of So Many'

FIGURE 42. Billy DeWolfe, Jr.'s, funeral service reported in the *Quincy Sun*, March 14, 1974

Figure 43. Wait staff of the Mount Washington Hotel, Bretton Woods, summer, 1944. Barbara DeWolfe is in the third row, fourth from left.

Figure 44. Young Grace DeWolfe (Holton), on left, with cousin Peggy, on right

Figure 45. Copy of a popular 1892 print, "All is Vanity," which hung in Aunt Grace's apartment

FIGURE 46. Eunice DeWolfe Copp playing Mabel's violin, circa 1978

Appendix: The Spanish Civil War

In 1898, Spain suffered a humiliating defeat by the United States in the Spanish-American War, which began with the sinking of the USS *Maine* in Havana Harbor.

Spain had long suffered from chronic instability. France, on the other hand, had, with the revolution of 1789, purged the nation of the ancient traditions and the accompanying corruption. Spain had kept its old customs, traditions—and corruptions—of the ancient monarchy, including the position of the Roman Catholic Church in the government.

In the early years of the twentieth century, Catholic Spain experienced much unrest. King Alfonso XIII was authoritarian and maintained a government of the church and of the elite and privileged. Increasing popular unrest forced the king to abdicate in 1930, and the Second Republic was declared. "The Republic had broad support in all segments of society. Elections in June 1931 returned a large majority of Republicans and Socialists to the government" ("Spanish Civil War," Wikipedia).

The Second Spanish Republic did not last long. Conservative and liberal factions went head-to-head. The conservatives were made up of the aristocrats and loyalists, faithful to the ancient system. Among the liberals, seeking democratic reform, were the communists, socialists, and nationalists.

A constitution, drawn up in 1936, made public education secular. This enraged the Catholic Church. Democracy was fragile, and on July 17, 1936, the Spanish Civil War began. "Open violence occurred in the streets of Spanish cities and militancy continued to increase" ("Spanish Civil War," Wikipedia).

Appendix: The Spanish Civil War

Joining the conservative forces was Francisco Franco, who in 1926 had become a brigadier general at the age of thirty-three. He soon took charge of the conservative forces. Italy and Nazi Germany sent troops and equipment to support Franco. Fighting went on for almost five bloody years. In April 1939, the Spanish Civil War was over. Franco's forces had won and he became a fascist, but not a Nazi. Franco was, in essence, dictator of Spain.

In October, 1940 Hitler met with Franco at Hendaye on the France-Spain border, but their conversation was inconclusive. At the end of the nine-hour meeting, Hitler admitted, "he would rather have three or four teeth pulled than talk with Franco again" (Pierson 1999, 160).

Franco had decided to stay neutral. The question of Gibraltar worried him. Gibraltar is situated strategically on the south tip of the Spanish peninsula. It had been ceded to England during the War of Spanish Succession. Therefore, England owned Gibraltar, known as "The Rock," which included a fortress. Franco's reluctance to allow the German army onto Spanish soil frustrated a German plan to capture the Rock ("Gibraltar," Wikipedia).

When Germany was defeated in 1945 at the end of World War II, Franco remained in power. In 1947, Franco established the Council of the Regency, which transitioned to democracy with the return of young Prince Juan Carlos. The general died in 1975.

References

Berg, A. Scott. *Wilson*. New York: Putnam, 2013.

Coetzee, Frans, and Marilyn Shevin-Coetzee. *World War I and European Society: A Sourcebook*. Lexington, MA: D. C. Heath, 1995.

Cullen, Frank, Florence Hackman, and Donald O'Neilly. *Vaudeville Old and New: An Encyclopedia of Variety Performers in America*, 2-vol ed. New York: Routledge, 2007.

Dowling, Robert M. *Eugene O'Neill: A Life in Four Acts*. New Haven: Yale University Press, 2014.

McAllister, Jim. "Jean Missud: Remembering Salem's Most Beloved Band Leader." *Welcome to Salem, Massachusetts, The City Guide*. N.p., n.d. Web. 25 June 2015. <http://www.salemweb.com/tales/missud.shtml>.

Pierson, Peter. *The History of Spain*. Westport, Connecticut: Greenwood Press, 1999.

Sobel, Bernard. *A Pictorial History of Vaudeville*. New York: Citadel Press, 1961.

Stanley, Raymond W. *The Four Thompsons of Boston Harbor: 1621–1965*. Boston, MA: privately printed, 1966.

About the Author

Richard Charles Tappan is a veteran educator, having taught English, literature, journalism, drama, and the writing process at the middle- and high-school levels for almost thirty years. He received his B.A. and a Master of Arts in Teaching from the University of New Hampshire. During the summers of 1993 through 1999, Tappan was a writing instructor in the Advanced Studies Program at St. Paul's School in Concord, New Hampshire. He was the drama director and English teacher at the Oyster River High School, Durham, New Hampshire, from 1981 until 2000, producing and directing ambitious stage productions, including an original musical that he co-wrote, depicting the life of Marie Antoinette leading up to the French Revolution.

In 1989, Tappan received the Merrill outstanding secondary educator award from Cornell University. After retiring from teaching, Tappan became an associate with the consulting firm, Center for Assessment, and was made project manager with Marge Petit for the Wyoming Consortium for the improvement of educational performance.

The novel *Voices from Cold River* is based on the life of Sarah Mariah Tappan, Richard Tappan's paternal grandmother. The novel was a finalist for the 2006 Peter Taylor Prize.

Tappan lives with his wife, Sally, in Dover, New Hampshire. They have three grown children and twelve grandchildren.

www.ingramcontent.com/pod-product-compliance
Lightning Source LLC
Chambersburg PA
CBHW071738090426
42738CB00011B/2518